TEACHER'S PET PUBLICATIONS

LITPLAN TEACHER PACK
for
I Heard the Owl Call My Name
based on the book by
Margaret Craven

Written by
Mary B. Collins

© 1995 Teacher's Pet Publications
All Rights Reserved

This **LitPlan** for Margaret Craven's
I Heard The Owl Call My Name
has been brought to you by Teacher's Pet Publications, Inc.

Copyright Teacher's Pet Publications 1995
11504 Hammock Point
Berlin MD 21811

Only the student materials in this unit plan (such as worksheets,
study questions, and tests) may be reproduced multiple times
for use in the purchaser's classroom.

For any additional copyright questions,
contact Teacher's Pet Publications.

www.tpet.com

TABLE OF CONTENTS - *I Heard the Owl Call My Name*

Introduction	4
Unit Objectives	6
Reading Assignment Sheet	7
Unit Outline	8
Study Questions (Short Answer)	11
Quiz/Study Questions (Multiple Choice)	20
Pre-reading Vocabulary Worksheets	37
Lesson One (Introductory Lesson)	51
Nonfiction Assignment Sheet	53
Oral Reading Evaluation Form	55
Writing Assignment 1	57
Writing Assignment 2	63
Writing Assignment 3	67
Writing Evaluation Form	66
Vocabulary Review Activities	61
Extra Writing Assignments/Discussion ?s	60
Unit Review Activities	68
Unit Tests	71
Unit Resource Materials	107
Vocabulary Resource Materials	123

INTRODUCTION - *I Heard The Owl Call My Name*

This unit has been designed to develop students' reading, writing, thinking, and language skills through exercises and activities related to *I Heard the Owl Call My Name* by Margaret Craven. It includes sixteen lessons, supported by extra resource materials.

The **introductory lesson** introduces students to one main theme of the novel by having a missionary come in to speak to the class about his/her work. Students are also given the materials they will be using during the unit.

The **reading assignments** are approximately thirty pages each; some are a little shorter while others are a little longer. Students have approximately 15 minutes of pre-reading work to do prior to each reading assignment. This pre-reading work involves reviewing the study questions for the assignment and doing some vocabulary work for 8 to 10 vocabulary words they will encounter in their reading.

The **study guide questions** are fact-based questions; students can find the answers to these questions right in the text. These questions come in two formats: short answer or multiple choice. The best use of these materials is probably to use the short answer version of the questions as study guides for students (since answers will be more complete), and to use the multiple choice version for occasional quizzes. It might be a good idea to make transparencies of your answer keys for the overhead projector.

The **vocabulary work** is intended to enrich students' vocabularies as well as to aid in the students' understanding of the book. Prior to each reading assignment, students will complete a two-part worksheet for approximately 8 to 10 vocabulary words in the upcoming reading assignment. Part I focuses on students' use of general knowledge and contextual clues by giving the sentence in which the word appears in the text. Students are then to write down what they think the words mean based on the words' usage. Part II nails down the definitions of the words by giving students dictionary definitions of the words and having students match the words to the correct definitions based on the words' contextual usage. Students should then have an understanding of the words when they meet them in the text.

After the reading assignments, students will go back and formulate answers for the study guide questions. Discussion of these questions serves as a **review** of the most important events and ideas presented in the reading assignments.

After students have read the novel and have an understanding of the literal level, a lesson is devoted to **the extra discussion questions/writing assignments**. These questions focus on interpretation, critical analysis and personal response, employing a variety of thinking skills and adding to the students' understanding of the novel.

There is also a **vocabulary review** lesson which pulls together all of the fragmented vocabulary lists for the reading assignments and gives students a review of all of the words they have studied.

There are three **writing assignments** in this unit, each with the purpose of informing, persuading, or having students express personal opinions. The first assignment is for personal opinions: students write their opinions about the assimilation of minority cultures into a dominant culture. The second assignment is to inform: students write a composition in which they state what they will say in their oral reports related to their **research assignment**. The third assignment is to persuade: students write a letter their congressman persuading him/her to either push for or go against the idea that minority cultures should keep their own languages as a predominant language in the areas where they have large populations.

In the **research assignment**, students are divided into three research groups: Group 1 researches Northwestern Indian tribes and cultures, Group 2 researches current affairs relating to Indian tribes, and Group 3 researches animals in Indian cultures.

There is a **nonfiction reading assignment** related to the research project and Writing Assignment 2, mentioned above. During one class period, students also make **oral presentations** about the nonfiction pieces they have read. This not only exposes all students to a wealth of information, it also gives students the opportunity to practice **public speaking**.

The **review lesson** pulls together all of the aspects of the unit. The teacher is given four or five choices of activities or games to use which all serve the same basic function of reviewing all of the information presented in the unit.

The **unit test** comes in two formats: multiple choice-matching-true/false or short answer. As a convenience, two different tests for each format have been included. In addition there is an Advanced Short Answer Unit Test for students who need more of a challenge.

There are additional **support materials** included with this unit. The **resource sections** include suggestions for an in-class library, crossword and word search puzzles related to the novel, and extra vocabulary worksheets. There is a list of **bulletin board ideas** which gives the teacher suggestions for bulletin boards to go along with this unit. In addition, there is a list of **extra class activities** the teacher could choose from to enhance the unit or as a substitution for an exercise the teacher might feel is inappropriate for his/her class. The **teacher's manual** has the answer keys for the worksheets, tests, puzzles, etc. The **student packet** has worksheets, tests, puzzles, etc. left blank for students to fill-in. Materials in the student packet may be reproduced for use in the teacher's classroom without infringement of copyrights. Teachers' manuals may not be reproduced without the written consent of Teacher's Pet Publications, Inc.

UNIT OBJECTIVES - *I Heard the Owl Call My Name*

1. Through reading Craven's *I Heard the Owl Call My Name*, students will study the effects of a modern culture on the old ways of the Indians.

2. Students will demonstrate their understanding of the text on four levels: factual, interpretive, critical and personal.

3. Students will study various North American Indian tribes and cultures.

4. Students will discuss the idea of assimilation of minority cultures into a dominant culture.

5. Students will discuss the positive and negative effects of having a multicultural society.

6. Students will be given the opportunity to practice reading aloud and silently to improve their skills in each area.

7. Students will answer questions to demonstrate their knowledge and understanding of the main events and characters in *I Heard the Owl Call My Name* as they relate to the author's theme development.

8. Students will enrich their vocabularies and improve their understanding of the novel through the vocabulary lessons prepared for use in conjunction with the novel.

9. The writing assignments in this unit are geared to several purposes:
    a. To have students demonstrate their abilities to inform, to persuade, or to express their own personal ideas
        Note: Students will demonstrate ability to write effectively to <u>inform</u> by developing and organizing facts to convey information. Students will demonstrate the ability to write effectively to <u>persuade</u> by selecting and organizing relevant information, establishing an argumentative purpose, and by designing an appropriate strategy for an identified audience. Students will demonstrate the ability to write effectively to <u>express personal ideas</u> by selecting a form and its appropriate elements.
    b. To check the students' reading comprehension
    c. To make students think about the ideas presented by the novel
    d. To encourage logical thinking
    e. To provide an opportunity to practice good grammar and improve students' use of the English language.

READING ASSIGNMENT SHEET - *I Heard the Owl Call My Name*

Date Assigned	Reading Assignment	Completion Date
	Chapters 1-3	
	Chapters 4-7	
	Chapters 8-11	
	Chapters 12-17	
	Chapters 18-23	

UNIT OUTLINE - *I Heard the Owl Call My Name*

1 Guest Speaker	2 PVR 1-3	3 Study ?s 1-3 PVR 4-7	4 Study ?s 4-7 PVR 8-11 W. A. #1	5 Study ?s 8-11 PVR 12-17 Library
6 Study ?s 12-17 PVR 18-23	7 Study ?s 18-23 Extra Discussion Questions	8 Vocabulary	9 Group Work	10 Writing Assignment #2
11 Nonfiction Reports	12 Nonfiction Reports	13 Discussion: Multicultural Society	14 Writing Assignment #3	15 Review
16 Test				

Key: P = Preview Study Questions   V = Vocabulary Work   R = Read

STUDY GUIDE QUESTIONS

SHORT ANSWER STUDY GUIDE QUESTIONS - *I Heard the Owl Call My Name*

Chapters 1-3
1. What information does the Preface reveal?
2. Why do you think Margaret Craven included the preface?
3. Who is Mark Brian?
4. Why does Caleb come out of retirement?
5. Before Mark meets the Indians, how does he think they will respond to him? Why?
6. How does Jim Wallace respond to Mark?
7. Identify the speaker: "If man were to vanish from this planet tomorrow, here he would leave no trace that he ever was."
8. What is a potlatch?
9. What English phrase does not exist in Kwakwala?
10. Why is the dead boy not buried?
11. Why has it taken so long for the RCMP officer to come and issue the burial permit?
12. What does it tell us about Mark that he "sensed there was something yet unfinished of which he had no part"?
13. What is a gluckaston?
14. Identify: "He will say we and he will mean us."
15. What is the villagers' first impression of their new vicar?
16. What is Mrs. Hudson's "small revenge on the white man, the intruder"?
17. What is Marta Stephens making for Mark?

Chapters 4-7
1. What is the condition of the church and the vicarage?
2. What advice does the Bishop write to Mark?
3. Identify: "There is a bear loose in the church."
4. What kind of man is the teacher?
5. What are the two kinds of naivete Mark quotes from Schweitzer?
6. Who are Mark's first friends?
7. What is the salmon called?
8. Why do you think "the watchful waiting left the Indian's eyes"?
9. What does Mark mean when he says the death of the swimmer is a triumph?
10. Why does Jim say Keetah will marry him instead of Gordon?
11. Why does Mark stop using the Victorian "we"?
12. How does Mark pull little Ethel's tooth?
13. Identify: "They are none of the things one has been led to believe."
14. Why does Mark say, "Yes, my lord"?

Owl Short Answer Study Questions Page 2

Chapters 8-11
1. What is the "strange little wind of dissent" that Mark feels?
2. Why is Mrs. Hudson upset?
3. Why is Mrs. Hudson's family leaving the village in shame?
4. Why does Mrs. Hudson say to Mark, "What have you done to us?"
5. What happened to Keetah's sister?
6. What does Mark promise Gordon's mother as she is dying?
7. Why does the Bishop write Mark, ". . . now you are theirs."

Chapters 12-17
1. How is the new vicarage transported up the river?
2. Why must the vicarage be finished before August?
3. What transforms the inlet into a "lovely city of lights"?
4. Identify: "The church belongs in the gutter. It is where it does some of its best work."
5. Describe the visitors who come to the village.
6. Where are Mark and Jim taking Gordon and the boys?
7. How does Mark feel with his sister and his college friends?
8. What concerns do the old men of the village bring to Mark?
9. What is Mark's solution to the state of the old burial ground?
10. How had Gordon changed?
11. What do the elders want Gordon to do?
12. What do the old people of the village fear in Gordon?
13. Why does Keetah leave with Gordon?
14. Why does Caleb come to Kingcome?

Chapters 18-23
1. What does Mark promise Calamity?
2. Why does Keetah return?
3. What reason does Keetah give for having Gordon's child?
4. Why does Marta write to the Bishop and tell him she "keeps her promise now"?
5. Why do you think the Bishop feels that it's "easier here, where only the fundamentals count, to learn . . . enough of the meaning of life to be ready to die"?
6. Why did Mark say to Marta, "On the bank of the river I heard the owl call my name"?
7. Is Mark more afraid of death or of leaving Kingcome?
8. What gift do the villagers offer Mark?
9. What does Mark ask Jim to do for Keetah?
10. What does Jim tell Keetah?
11. Why does Mrs. Hudson decide to have carrots?
12. How is Mark's death, like the swimmer's, a triumph?

ANSWER KEY SHORT ANSWER STUDY GUIDE QUESTIONS
I Heard the Owl Call My Name

<u>Chapters 1-3</u>

1. What information does the Preface reveal?

    The young ordained has only a few years to live and he will spend them serving Indian villages. The Bishop describes Kingcome as his hardest parish, yet it is where he would go if he were in the young man's place.

2. Why do you think Margaret Craven included the preface?

    It sparks the reader's curiosity and foreshadows the story. The reader senses or infers that many challenges will confront the dying vicar. Something tragic is going to happen, but something wonderful will happen, too.

3. Who is Mark Brian?

    He is the young, ordained man sent to Kingcome.

4. Why does Caleb come out of retirement?

    He comes to teach Mark how to run and maintain the diesel launch and to acquaint Mark with some of the Indian customs and characteristics.

5. Before Mark meets the Indians, how does he think they will respond to him? Why?

    He thinks they will respond to him with arrogance because he has heard of their intelligence and their lavish feasts where gifts are distributed to all guests by the host chief who wishes to impress upon them his great wealth.

6. How does Jim Wallace respond to Mark?

    With eyes full of quiet pride and deep sadness, Jim accepts Mark's handshake but returns no pressure.

7. Identify the speaker: "If man were to vanish from this planet tomorrow, here he would leave no trace that he ever was."

    Mark was describing the awesome grandeur and beauty of the British Columbian coast.

8. What is a potlatch?

    It is a feast with gifts given by the leader of one Indian tribe to another tribe in order to impress his wealth and status upon the neighboring tribe.

9. What English phrase does not exist in Kwakwala?

    "Thank you" does not exist in Kwakwala.

10. Why is the dead boy not buried?
    The tribe must wait until a burial permit is issued by the RCMP.

11. Why has it taken so long for the RCMP officer to come and issue the burial permit?
    Evidently, he has waited for a fair day so that he could bring his girlfriend.

12. What does it tell us about Mark that he "sensed there was something yet unfinished of which he had no part"?
    It illustrates his respect and consideration for the traditions and values of the Indians.

13. What is a gluckaston?
    It is a mixture of seaweed and corn which has been left at the vicarage for Mark and Jim to eat.

14. Identify: "He will say we and he will mean us."
    Jim is discussing Mark with Chief Eddy. He is referring to Mark's use of the Victorian "we" in asking Jim what needs to be done. It appears that the Indians are familiar with people using the word "we" when they want the Indians to do something for them.

15. What is the villagers' first impression of their new vicar?
    They realize that he does not have the skills to live in the village without help; he cannot hunt or fish and knows very little about his boat, but they are pleased that he has shown respect for their customs.

16. What is Mrs. Hudson's "small revenge on the white man, the intruder"?
    She makes mashed turnips for dinner because she believes that the white men hate them.

17. What is Marta Stephens making for Mark?
    She is making him a warm hat.

Chapters 4-7

1. What is the condition of the church and the vicarage?
    Both buildings are full of holes, leaks, rotten floors and moldy walls. They both need to be replaced.

2. What advice does the Bishop write to Mark?
    He suggests that he must work with his hands to gain the respect of the Indians.

3. Identify: "There is a bear loose in the church."
    Mrs. Hudson is describing Mark's sweeping and scrubbing.

4. What kind of man is the teacher?

    He is selfish and inconsiderate. He is not interested in the Indians or their culture; he is merely accumulating the "hardship points" so he can earn a grant to study in Greece. He is not a wise man or he would realize his opportunity to learn from the Indians.

5. What are the two kinds of naivete Mark quotes from Schweitzer?

    One kind of naivete is not even being aware that there exists a problem or situation. The other kind is the naivete of a man who has searched for answers and discovered that man knows little, yet he retains his convictions and beliefs.

6. Who are Mark's first friends?

    Two small children are his first friends.

7. What is the salmon called?

    The salmon is called "swimmer."

8. Why do you think "the watchful waiting left the Indian's eyes"?

    Mark quoted an old Indian prayer that Jim had forgotten. This made Jim take an interest in Mark as more than just the new vicar who must be accommodated. Jim looks at Mark as another man and potential friend after this exchange because Mark has shown his real interest in the people and their ways.

9. What does Mark mean when he says the death of the swimmer is a triumph?

    He means that the salmon has lived its life and exhausted its energy completely for the purpose it was created. It has returned to spawn and die as God intended. Its life is a success, not a sadness.

10. Why does Jim say Keetah will marry him instead of Gordon?

    Gordon is "fast moving water" while "Keetah is the pool." In other words, they are not well suited for each other even though arrangements have already been made.

11. Why does Mark stop using the Victorian "we"?

    He and Jim are friends and speak to each other as equals. He realizes that using the "we" is not appropriate.

12. How does Mark pull little Ethel's tooth?

    He ties a string to it and a door and slams the door shut.

13. Identify: "They are none of the things one has been led to believe."

    Mark is describing the Indians in a letter to his Bishop.

14. Why does Mark say, "Yes, my lord"?
> He is acknowledging his commitment to his parish.

Chapters 8-11

1. What is the "strange little wind of dissent" that Mark feels?
> It is the tension between the old ways and traditions of the elders and the new "outside world" ways the children bring back to the village from school.

2. Why is Mrs. Hudson upset?
> Her granddaughter has written to her that she intends to marry a white man.

3. Why is Mrs. Hudson's family leaving the village in shame?
> Her granddaughter and the white man have bought the valuable mask from Gordon's uncle after getting him drunk. They are shamed that the girl was a part of such duplicity.

4. Why does Mrs. Hudson say to Mark, "What have you done to us?"
> She is speaking to Mark, the white man, not Mark the vicar who is becoming a part of the village life. Mrs. Hudson's granddaughter returned to the village in the clothes and make-up of the white world, and with her white man, she practically stole a part of the villagers' pride and heritage. Mrs. Hudson is taking out her frustrations about the new ways taking over the old.

5. What happened to Keetah's sister?
> The white man deserted her in Vancouver, where she died within three months. The world of a town was completely alien to her, and her only course of survival was to prostitute herself and bury her shame and despair in alcohol and drugs.

6. What does Mark promise Gordon's mother as she is dying?
> He promises that he will help Gordon get an education.

7. Why does the Bishop write Mark, ". . . now you are theirs."
> The Indians have completely accepted Mark through his suffering with them. He has become a real part of the village.

Chapters 12-17

1. How is the new vicarage transported up the river?
> Mark and the Indians use a forestry barge to transport the materials.

2. Why must the vicarage be finished before August?
> The rains come then; also in August the Indians will be allowed to buy liquor.

3. What transforms the inlet into a "lovely city of lights"?
   The salmon fishermen drifting in their lighted boats transforms the inlet.

4. Identify: "The church belongs in the gutter. It is where it does some of its best work."
   The Bishop is telling Mark that the "gutter" is often where the people are who need the church the most.

5. Describe the visitors who come to the village.
   The California group questioned Mark about the villagers as though they were merely interesting objects for their entertainment. The English woman had studied their culture, yet still only saw the Indians as objects of her study. Neither saw the Indians as being human.

6. Where are Mark and Jim taking Gordon and the boys?
   They are taking them to Vancouver to begin school.

7. How does Mark feel with his sister and his college friends?
   He feels out of touch and not able to relate to their lives in towns and cities.

8. What concerns do the old men of the village bring to Mark?
   The old grave yard where "coffins" are hoisted up in trees is in terrible shape. The Coffins have fallen, rotted, and come open so that the bones of their ancestors are on the ground.

9. What is Mark's solution to the state of the old burial ground?
   He suggests that they clear the area and excavate one mass grave for all the ancestors. Thus, they will be together and at peace, properly buried.

10. How had Gordon changed?
    He had become more like the white man in dress and speech and especially in his aspirations.

11. What do the elders want Gordon to do?
    They want him to return to the village and the traditional Indian life, in effect to choose the old ways and renounce his modern education and goals.

12. What do the old people of the village fear in Gordon?
    They fear his desire to become an educated and professional man and therefore not a part of the village community. They are afraid of the end of their identity as a people. They are afraid that their village is dying.

13. Why does Keetah leave with Gordon?
    She is to be his wife and will try to live in the world outside the village.

14. Why does Caleb come to Kingcome?
    He wants Mark to realize that soon the Indians and their way of life will disappear or become absorbed and lost in the modern world.

<u>Chapters 18-23</u>

1. What does Mark promise Calamity?
    He promises him that he will spread his ashes on Knight's Inlet.

2. Why does Keetah return?
    She cannot adjust to the white man's world; she has known and loved her village ways for too long. She realizes that although Gordon has become very "white," she will always remain an Indian.

3. What reason does Keetah give for having Gordon's child?
    A part of Gordon will remain in the village.

4. Why does Marta write to the Bishop and tell him she "keeps her promise now"?
    Marta sees that Mark's health is failing and notifies the Bishop as has apparently been prearranged.

5. Why do you think the Bishop feels that it's "easier here, where only the fundamentals count, to learn . . . enough of the meaning of life to be ready to die"?
    Although life is primitive in the villages, it encompasses all the human needs: love, work, play, death, hope, etc. The struggles of human life are clearer in this setting, as are the achievements.

6. Why did Mark say to Marta, "On the bank of the river I heard the owl call my name"?
    He senses he is seriously ill and dying and wants to know if it is true.

7. Is Mark more afraid of death or of leaving Kingcome?
    He fears leaving his home more.

8. What gift do the villagers offer Mark?
    They offer him a place to die in peace with friends and family; they ask him to remain with them.

9. What does Mark ask Jim to do for Keetah?
    He asks him to treat her as a partner in life, to be polite to her, and to take her out into the world so she will get used to it.

10. What does Jim tell Keetah?

> He tells her that he will let her plan their house, that he will not pound the table for more coffee, that he will not leave her alone too often and that he will taker her out into the world so that she can get used to it. He gives her the promise he made Mark.

11. Why does Mrs. Hudson decide to have carrots?

> She thinks she has been a stubborn woman for serving turnips for so many years. The white man's arrival is inevitable; it is a concession she makes to begin accepting the new way of life, and it is in a way a tribute to Mark.

12. How is Mark's death, like the swimmer's, a triumph?

> He lived a short yet full, rich life. Like the swimmer, he died in a triumph of achievement. His purpose was fulfilled.

MULTIPLE CHOICE STUDY GUIDE/QUIZ QUESTIONS - *I Heard the Owl Call My Name*

Chapters 1-3

1. What information does the preface reveal?
    a. It explains the Indian culture.
    b. It tells about the priest's life before he came to the village.
    c. It tells about the young vicar's illness.
    d. It tells why the author wrote the book.

2. True or False: The preface sparks the reader's curiosity and foreshadows the story?
    a. True
    b. False

3. Who is Mark Brian?
    a. He is the narrator of the story.
    b. He is the bishop.
    c. He is the young ordained man.
    d. He is the Indian chief.

4. Why does Caleb come out of retirement?
    a. He misses his old duties and wants to return to them.
    b. He is out of money and must work again to support himself.
    c. He has been ordered to do so by the bishop.
    d. He wants to teach Mark about the boat and the Indian customs.

5. Before Mark meets the Indians, how does he think they will respond to him?
    a. He thinks they will be arrogant.
    b. He thinks they will be wary and unfriendly.
    c. He thinks they will be cautious but congenial.
    d. He thinks they will be very friendly.

6. How does Jim Wallace respond to Mark?
    a. He smiles and shakes Mark's hand several times.
    b. He ignores Mark completely.
    c. He accepts Mark's handshake but returns no pressure.
    d. He smiles and says hello, but refuses to have any physical contact.

I Heard the Owl Call My Name Multiple Choice Study Questions Page 2

7. Identify the speaker: "If man were to vanish from this planet tomorrow, here he would leave no trace that he ever was."
    a. It was the bishop.
    b. It was Caleb.
    c. It was Jim.
    d. It was Mark.

8. What is a potlach?
    a. It is a feast with gifts given by the leader of one tribe to another to impress them with his wealth.
    b. It is a type of Indian dwelling that is warm in the winter and cool in the summer. The Indians have built one for Mark.
    c. It is a ritual dance done to welcome a newcomer and wish him good luck.
    d. It is a council meeting of the Indian chiefs, the priests, and the government officials, when tribal business is discussed.

9. What English phrase does not exist in Kwakwala?
    a. "I love you" does not exist.
    b. "The Great Spirit" does not exist.
    c. "Thank you" does not exist.
    d. "Honor thy father and thy mother" does not exist.

10. Why is the dead boy not buried?
    a. The priest has not yet said the funeral Mass.
    b. The tribe must wait until a burial permit has been issued by the RCMP.
    c. He has to be examined by the coroner to make sure he did not have any contagious diseases.
    d. His family cannot afford to buy a burial plot.

11. True or False: The RCMP officer has not yet come to the village because he has a broken leg and cannot travel.
    a. True
    b. False

I Heard the Owl Call My Name Multiple Choice Study Questions Page 3

12. What does it tell us about Mark that he "sensed there was something yet unfinished of which he had no part?"
    a. It illustrates his respect and consideration for the traditions and values of the Indians.
    b. It shows that he is a very fearful, almost paranoid, person.
    c. It shows that he does not make friends easily.
    d. It shows that he is a procrastinator; he has trouble completing a task.

13. What is a gluckaston?
    a. It is the sound the Indians make when they are hunting fowl. It resembles the sound the wild birds make to call their mates.
    b. It is a type of canoe that the Indians designed to be used in the treacherous waters near the village.
    c. It is a mixture of seaweed and corn which has been left at the vicarage for Mark and Jim to eat.
    d. It is a warm winter coat made by the Indian women. They have given one to Mark.

14. Identify the speaker: "He will say we and he will mean us."
    a. Jim is discussing Mark with Chief Eddy.
    b. Caleb is discussing the bishop with Mark.
    c. Mark is discussing Jim with Caleb.
    d. Chief Eddy is discussing Jim with Mrs. Hudson.

15. True or False: When the villagers realize that Mark does not have the skills to live in the village without help, they ask the bishop to send a replacement.
    a. True
    b. False

16. What is Mrs. Hudson's "small revenge on the white man, the intruder"?
    a. She always starches the bedsheets to make them uncomfortable.
    b. She does the housecleaning early in the morning to wake them up.
    c. She makes mashed turnips for dinner because she thinks white men hate turnips.
    d. She will only speak to them in the Indian language.

17. What is Marta Stephens making for Mark?
    a. She is making him a dictionary of Indian terms so he can talk to them.
    b. She is making his favorite dinner once a week.
    c. She is making a map of the area.
    d. She is making him a warm hat.

I Heard the Owl Call My Name Multiple Choice Study Questions Page 4

Chapters 4-7

18. What is the condition of the church and the vicarage?
    a. They are in excellent shape.
    b. They are full of holes, rotten floors, and moldy walls.
    c. They have recently been repaired.
    d. They were never repaired after a fire the previous year.

19. What advice does the Bishop write to Mark?
    a. The bishop suggests Mark must work with his hands to gain the respect of the Indians.
    b. He tells Mark to hire some white men to help with the project.
    c. He tells Mark to let the Indians do all of the work.
    d. He suggests that Mark leave everything the way it is for at least six months, until the Indians are used to him.

20. Identify "There is a bear loose in the church."
    a. Caleb means that one of the Indians is drunk and going berserk in the church.
    b. The Chief believes that the Great Spirit sent a bear, the symbol of good luck, to protect the church.
    c. Jim is explaining that most of the Indians get angry at having a church in the village.
    d. Mrs. Hudson is describing Mark's sweeping and scrubbing.

21. Which of the following statements does not describe the teacher?
    a. He is selfish and inconsiderate.
    b. He is not interested in the Indians or their culture.
    c. He is not a wise man.
    d. He is a drunkard and a gambler.

22. What word is missing in this statement of Mark's? "One kind of _____ is not even being aware that a problem exists. The other kind is the _____ of a man who has searched for answers and discovered that man knows little, yet he retains his convictions and beliefs."
    a. Selfishness
    b. Question
    c. Naivete
    d. Sin

I Heard the Owl Call My Name Multiple Choice Study Questions Page 5

23. Who are Mark's first friends?
    a. Two small children are his first friends.
    b. The schoolteachers are his first friends.
    c. The dogs are his first friends.
    d. The doctor and the shopkeeper are his first friends.

24. What is the salmon called?
    a. It is called "pink flesh."
    b. It is called "swimmer."
    c. It is called "wise one."
    d. It is called "provider."

25. What happened when Mark quoted an old Indian prayer that Jim had forgotten?
    a. Jim got upset and told Mark never to speak the holy words of the Indians.
    b. Jim accepted him as a potential friend because of Mark's interest in the people.
    c. Jim got a frightened look on his face and ran away.
    d. Jim was insulted and embarrassed.

26. True or False: Jim says the death of the salmon is a defeat.
    a. True
    b. False

27. What does Jim mean when he calls Gordon "fast moving water" and Keetah "the pool?"
    a. He thinks they will be a good match for each other.
    b. He thinks they are not well suited for each other.
    c. These are Gordon and Keetah's other Indian names.
    d. These are the roles Gordon and Keetah have in a tribal ritual.

28. How does Mark show that he thinks of Jim as an equal?
    a. He stops using the Victorian "we."
    b. He invites Jim to dinner.
    c. He asks Jim's advice on a few matters.
    d. He speaks to Jim in the Indian language.

29. How does Mark pull little Ethel's tooth?
    a. He wraps a towel around it and yanks.
    b. He gives her a large wad of chewing gum and she pulls it out herself while chewing.
    c. He ties a string to it and a door and slams the door shut.
    d. He doesn't. He tells her to wait and it will fall out when it is ready to.

I Heard the Owl Call My Name Multiple Choice Study Questions Page 6

30. True or false: In a letter to the Bishop about the Indians, Mark says, "They are none of the things one has been led to believe."
    a. True
    b. False

31. What does Mark say to acknowledge his commitment to his parish?
    a. He says, "So be it."
    b. He says, "Thy will be done."
    c. He says, "Your wish is my command."
    d. He says, "Yes, my lord."

I Heard the Owl Call My Name Multiple Choice Study Questions Page 7

Chapters 8-11

32. What is the "strange little wind of dissent" that Mark feels?
    a. A winter blizzard is approaching.
    b. It is the tension between the old ways and the new.
    c. He thinks the Bishop is displeased with his work.
    d. He had a disagreement with Jim and is worried that their friendship is in jeopardy.

33. Why is Mrs. Hudson upset?
    a. She has no one to chop the wood for her stove.
    b. The supplies will be a month late and she is worried that she will run out of food.
    c. Her sister has just died.
    d. Her granddaughter has written saying she is going to marry a white man.

34. Why is Mrs. Hudson's family leaving the village in shame?
    a. Her granddaughter and the white man are living together before they are married, and this is not permitted.
    b. Her granddaughter and the white man have bought the valuable mask from Gordon's uncle after getting him drunk.
    c. The white man has ridiculed the Indians' customs and refused to have any of them at his wedding.
    d. The white man is a gambler and the Indians do not play cards. They think it is evil.

35. True or False: When Mrs. Hudson talks to Mark and says "What have you done to us?" she is blaming him for her misfortune.
    a. True
    b. False

36. What happened to Keetah's sister?
    a. She lived with the white man for a few years, but left him to marry an Indian.
    b. She became the first Indian woman admitted to the University of British Columbia.
    c. She was deserted by the white man and died of alcohol and drug abuse.
    d. She returned home, humiliated, asking forgiveness.

37. What does Mark promise Gordon's mother as she is dying?
    a. He promises he will make sure Gordon is fed and taken care of.
    b. He promises he will help Gordon get an education.
    c. He promises he will find a wife for Gordon.
    d. He promises he will save Gordon's soul.

I Heard the Owl Call My Name Multiple Choice Study Questions Page 8

38. What does the Bishop write to Mark?
    a. "You are now theirs."
    b. "You will never truly be one with them."
    c. "Your time will soon be done."
    d. "Have faith."

I Heard the Owl Call My Name Multiple Choice Study Questions Page 9

<u>Chapters 12-17</u>

39. How is the new vicarage transported to its site?
    a. The Indians carry it piece by piece on their backs overland.
    b. It is dropped in by helicopter.
    c. Mark and the Indians use a forestry barge to transport the materials.
    d. Caleb uses the diesel launch, and makes several trips over a two week period.

40. True or False: The vicarage must be finished before August when the rains come.
    a. True
    b. False

41. What transforms the inlet into a "lovely city of lights?"
    a. The village has just received electricity, and all of the houses have their lights on.
    b. The Indians have lit campfires all along the shore to welcome visitors.
    c. The Aurora Borealis is shining in the night sky.
    d. The salmon fishermen have their boats lit up.

42. Where does the Bishop say the church belongs, because it does some of its best work there?
    a. It belongs in the city.
    b. It belongs in the wilderness.
    c. It belongs in the gutter.
    d. It belongs in the North Country.

43. Which statement describes the visitors who come to the village?
    a. They were interested primarily in the Indians as human beings.
    b. They were interested in the Indians as objects of study and amusement, not as people.
    c. They were tourists just interested in finding a good fishing spot.
    d. They were desperate for food and shelter.

44. Where are Mark and Jim taking Gordon and the boys?
    a. They are going to the department store in town to buy new clothes.
    b. They are going on a hunting and fishing trip.
    c. They are going to the city to meet the Bishop.
    d. They are going to Vancouver to begin school.

I Heard the Owl Call My Name Multiple Choice Study Questions Page 10

45. How does Mark feel with his sister and his college friends?
    a. He feels holy and beyond them.
    b. He feels comfortable and secure.
    c. He feels out of touch and not able to relate to their lives.
    d. He feels reserved because he has not seen them for a long time.

46. True or False: The old men are concerned because the grave yard is in terrible shape. The coffins have fallen, rotted, and come open so that the bones of their ancestors are on the ground.
    a. True
    b. False

47. True or False: Mark suggests that they cremate the remains in the burial ground and scatter the ashes over the water.
    a. True
    b. False

48. What is Gordon like?
    a. He has become more like the white men in dress and speech and aspirations.
    b. He has retained his Indian ways.
    c. He is like an angry bear.
    d. He is like a cunning fox.

49. True or False: The elders are very supportive of Gordon's personal goals.
    a. True
    b. False

50. How do the old people of the village feel about Gordon?
    a. They accept him for who he is.
    b. They are jealous of him.
    c. They fear him and his ideas.
    d. They are not particularly concerned. They think he is a foolish young man who will come to his senses.

51. What does Keetah do?
    a. She leaves with Gordon to be his wife and live in the outside world.
    b. She remains behind in the village and looks for a new mate.
    c. She goes off on her own in the wilderness to pray and meditate to help her decide what to do.
    d. She writes to her friend to ask advice.

I Heard the Owl Call My Name Multiple Choice Study Questions Page 11

52. Why does Caleb come to Kingcome?
    a. He brings a special communication from the Bishop.
    b. He comes to help Mark repair the vicarage.
    c. He is lonely and comes for company.
    d. He wants Mark to realize that the Indians and their way of life may soon disappear.

I Heard the Owl Call My Name Multiple Choice Study Questions Page 12

<u>Chapters 18-23</u>

53. What does Mark promise Calamity?
    a. He promises that he will take care of his family.
    b. He promises to say the Last Rites as well as the Indian prayers.
    c. He promises to plant a tree near his grave every year on the anniversary of his death.
    d. He promises to spread his ashes on Knight's Inlet.

54. What happens to Keetah?
    a. She adjusts to her new life and prospers.
    b. She cannot adjust to her new life and returns to her old ways.
    c. She dies in the big city.
    d. She becomes ill and must postpone her trip.

55. How does Keetah insure that Gordon will remain a part of the village?
    a. She keeps his last name as her own.
    b. She brings photographs of him.
    c. She has his child.
    d. She insists that he visit her twice a year.

56. Marta writes to the Bishop and tells him she is "keeping her promise now." What is her promise?
    a. She has agreed to stay at the vicarage until she retires.
    b. She has trained the young village girls to be good housewives.
    c. She has notified the Bishop that Mark's health is failing.
    d. She has converted to Christianity.

57. What does the Bishop think about life in the villages?
    a. He thinks village life is much more difficult than life elsewhere because of the lack of conveniences.
    b. He thinks the struggles and achievements of life are clearer in the village.
    c. He dismisses it without much thought.
    d. He wonders if anyone there will ever be converted to Christianity.

58. Why did Mark say to Marta, "On the bank of the river I heard the owl call my name?"
    a. He was delirious with a fever and didn't know what he was talking about.
    b. He was explaining that he finally felt accepted into the village.
    c. He sensed that he was dying and wanted to know if it were true.
    d. He was talking symbolically about the blending of the old customs and the modern way of life. He felt like he was the bridge between the two.

I Heard the Owl Call My Name Multiple Choice Study Questions Page 13

59. Of what is Mark more afraid?
    a. He is more afraid of death.
    b. He is more afraid of leaving his home in Kingcome.
    c. He is more afraid of the Indian spirits.
    d. He is more afraid of being alone.

60. What gift do the villagers offer Mark?
    a. They name the newest born male child after him.
    b. They offer him a place to die in peace with friends and family.
    c. They offer to pay his passage back to the city.
    d. They begin to attend church regularly.

61. Which of the following is not one of the things Mark asks Jim to do for Keetah?
    a. He asks Jim to send her to school in the city.
    b. He asks Jim to treat her as a partner in life.
    c. He asks Jim to be polite to her.
    d. He asks Jim to take her out into the world so she can get used to it.

62. What does Jim do about Mark's request?
    a. He refuses to honor it, because it goes against the old ways.
    b. He does everything Mark asks.
    c. He writes to the Bishop.
    d. He listens to Mark's request, but he can't do it.

63. How does Mrs. Hudson show her acceptance of the white man and the new way of life?
    a. She lets the white visitors use the front door instead of admitting them through the kitchen.
    b. She speaks to them in English.
    c. She serves carrots for dinner.
    d. She smiles and calls them by name.

64. Which of the following statements describes Mark's life/death?
    a. He lived a short yet full, rich life. He died in a triumph of achievement like the swimmer.
    b. He lived only through others, like the reflection on the water.
    c. His life was hollow, like the wind.
    d. His death was sudden, like a flame being extinguished.

ANSWER KEY - MULTIPLE CHOICE STUDY/QUIZ QUESTIONS
I Heard the Owl Call My Name

Chapters 1-3	Chapters 4-7	Chapters 8-11	Chapters 12-17	Chapters 18-23
1. C	18. B	32. B	39. C	53. D
2. A	19. A	33. D	40. A	54. B
3. B	20. D	34. B	41. D	55. C
4. D	21. D	35. B	42. C	56. C
5. A	22. C	36. C	43. B	57. B
6. C	23. A	37. B	44. D	58. C
7. D	24. B	38. A	45. C	59. B
8. A	25. B		46. A	60. B
9. C	26. B		47. B	61. A
10. B	27. B		48. A	62. B
11. B	28. A		49. B	63. C
12. A	29. C		50. C	64. A
13. C	30. A		51. A	
14. A	31. D		52. D	
15. B				
16. C				
17. D				

PREREADING VOCABULARY WORKSHEETS

VOCABULARY - *I Heard the Owl Call My Name*

<u>Chapters 1 - 3</u> Part I: Using Prior Knowledge and Contextual Clues

Below are the sentences in which the vocabulary words appear in the text. Read the sentence. Use any clues you can find in the sentence combined with your prior knowledge, and write what you think the underlined words mean in the space provided.

1. Caleb, the old canon, had come out of retirement to acquaint him with all the endearing--and <u>exasperating</u>--little ways of the forty-foot diesel launch upon which his life would depend.

2. Because Caleb was old, the young man had thought, of course, he would be <u>garrulous</u> and full of reminiscence, but he was wrong.

3. Now Kingcome is known as a compact, Christian village, and this means that to run smoothly the elected chief, the <u>vicar</u> and the agent from the Indian Affairs Department must be co-operative and wise, and though I am sure the Lord could pass a small miracle and manage this, He seldom does.

4. Now it occurred to Mark that every single thing that went to Kingcome had to be taken up the river and for the first time he knew the stolid, stubborn indifference of the <u>inanimate.</u>

5. "Let's go in. I'll want an <u>autopsy.</u>"

6. When dark came to the village there was a gentle, cautious <u>confabulation</u> about the young vicar who had come from the great outside world.

7. Her face was finely wrinkled and of obvious <u>gentility</u>.

8. Ellie went willingly to the bed of any man who <u>beckoned</u> her, and since, at thirteen years, brutality was all she knew of masculine attention, she liked best the man who mistreated her the most.

I Heard The Owl Vocabulary Chapters 1-3 Continued

Part II: Determining the Meaning - Match the vocabulary words to their dictionary definitions.

___ 1. exasperating
___ 2. garrulous
___ 3. vicar
___ 4. inanimate
___ 5. autopsy
___ 6. confabulation
___ 7. gentility
___ 8. beckoned

A. qualities appropriate to those well born, as self-respect, dignity, courage, courtesy
B. inflaming the anger of; making more grievous
C. familiar conversation; chat
D. summoned by a gesture, as a nod or motion of the finger
E. talking much
F. lifeless
G. clergyman; priest
H. dissection of a dead body to learn cause of death

Vocabulary - *I Heard the Owl Call My Name* Chapters 4 - 7

Part I: Using Prior Knowledge and Contextual Clues

Below are the sentences in which the vocabulary words appear in the text. Read the sentence. Use any clues you can find in the sentence combined with your prior knowledge, and write what you think the underlined words mean in the space provided.

1. Mark read it twice and had a sudden and <u>appalling</u> vision of hundreds of boards, kegs of nails, bolts and shingles, perhaps even a bathtub, all heavy, stubborn and totally inanimate, piled high on the float, waiting to be carried up the river by canoe.

2. And what did he know of himself here where loneliness was an <u>unavoidable</u> element of life, and a man must rely solely on himself?

3. Also, the teacher accosted him on the path, asking that he <u>intervene</u> with the authorities that he be given proper supplies.

4. The vicar might as well know right now that as for himself, he was an atheist; he considered Christianity a <u>calamity</u>.

5. Often in the first weeks, Mark was beset by a sense of <u>futility</u> and always he was lonely.

6. "Have you had sufficient <u>sustenance</u> to suffice?"

7. A week later one of the boys of the village was very ill in the night with what Mark was sure was <u>acute</u> appendicitis.

8. He walked slowly down the center aisle, and not wanting to open the door until the very last minute for fear of losing the <u>precious</u> heat, he walked to the window at the left of the door and stepped without expectation into one of those moments that is suspended . . . .

I Heard The Owl Vocabulary Chapters 4-7 Continued

Part II: Determining the Meaning - Match the vocabulary words to their dictionary definitions.

____ 9. appalling
____ 10. unavoidable
____ 11. intervene
____ 12. calamity
____ 13. futility

____ 14. sustenance
____ 15. acute
____ 16. precious

A. uselessness
B. of great value
C. misfortune; affliction; disaster
D. to come between
E. to cause consternation; cause to be overcome with fear or horror
F. cannot keep away from
G. food, nourishment; means of support
H. constituting a crisis; crucial

Vocabulary - *I Heard the Owl Call My Name* Chapters 8 - 11

Part I: Using Prior Knowledge and Contextual Clues

Below are the sentences in which the vocabulary words appear in the text. Read the sentence. Use any clues you can find in the sentence combined with your prior knowledge, and write what you think the underlined words mean in the space provided.

1. . . . . Mark felt a strange little wind of <u>dissent</u> which seemed to whisper in the firs, to precede him, to follow him wherever he went.

2. My people are proud of them, and <u>resent</u> them.

3. Through it all the Indians sat without sound or movement, <u>utterly</u> attentive.

4. They <u>taunted</u> each other, fingers to noses, and this time the audience shrieked with laughter, taunting each in turn, and applauding the favourite.

5. Once they were like the coronations of a king, or the <u>inauguration</u> of a president.

6. Farther down the river's bank they saw a group of the oldsters packing one of the larger canoes with great bundles of clothing as if for a long <u>trek</u>.

7. They belonged to the great and small hegiras of the self-<u>exiles</u> of this earth, clinging fiercely to a way that is almost gone, as the last leaves fall at last gently and with great pride.

8. In the cold, blustery days of February and March, when the men could not <u>pursue</u> the fish and the game, the life of the tribe turned in upon itself.

9. . . .and when Ellie's mother sat sewing with the other women, totally unresponsive, in her <u>vague</u>, sweet way, Mark knew also that she was probably in a drunken stupor because Sam had beat her again.

I Heard The Owl Vocabulary Chapters 8-11 Continued

10. At the headquarters of the RCMP Mark discussed the problem of Ellie with the sergeant in charge of the detachment, a man past middle age and wise, and from him Mark learned that to take Ellie from her parents without their <u>consent</u> was not easy.

Part II: Determining the Meaning - Match the vocabulary words to their dictionary definitions.

____ 17. dissent   A. a journey; a migration of a group in wagons
____ 18. resent   B. indefinite; confused, hazy
____ 19. utterly   C. to agree; to give approval
____ 20. taunted   D. to differ in opinion; disagreement
____ 21. inauguration   E. persons banished from their own country
____ 22. trek   F. to feel or express indignant displeasure
____ 23. exiles   G. to follow or chase; to seek
____ 24. pursue   H. jeered at; ridiculed; teased; insulted
____ 25. vague   I. completely, totally
____ 26. consent   J. formal installation into office

Vocabulary - *I Heard the Owl Call My Name* Chapters 12 - 17

Part I: Using Prior Knowledge and Contextual Clues

Below are the sentences in which the vocabulary words appear in the text. Read the sentence. Use any clues you can find in the sentence combined with your prior knowledge, and write what you think the underlined words mean in the space provided.

1. Sometimes Mark was <u>appalled</u> at how much was gone, how little they remembered from their long past, ...

2. When Gordon returned to the fishing, the elders returned, Keetah's dark head bent again to her notebook, and Jim <u>reasserting</u> the old role of the tribal male, pounding on the table when he wished coffee, and Keetah, putting down her pen to wait on him without a look, without a word.

3. . . . an English woman <u>anthropologist</u> came to visit the village, housed, by arrangements of the Indian Agent with a couple who were among the very few of the tribe who were not Christians and did not go to church.

4. On the way back to the boat they passed three young Indians, loud spoken, ill-kempt and slovenly, and he felt the boys stiffen with <u>enmity.</u>

5. And how did he handle the growing materialism in which so many people feel no need of faith and consider the church almost an <u>anachronism</u>?

6. They hunted the sea, and the sea <u>teemed</u> with fish, the woods were full of game and berries, and the air with fowl.

7. And suddenly the place became <u>eerie</u>, as if eyes were watching us, the silence filled with voices we felt but couldn't hear.

8. The old priest looked <u>abashed.</u>

I Heard The Owl Vocabulary Chapters 12-17 Continued

Part II: Determining the Meaning - Match the vocabulary words to their dictionary definitions.

___ 27. appalled
___ 28. reasserting
___ 29. anthropologist
___ 30. enmity
___ 31. anachronism
___ 32. teemed
___ 33. eerie
___ 34. abashed

A. abounded; crowded
B. one who studies the science of man
C. embarrassed
D. hostility; hatred; rancor
E. depressed; dismayed; overcome with fear or horror
F. reclaiming one's rights or position
G. out of place in point of time
H. weird; uncanny; serving to inspire fear

Vocabulary - *I Heard the Owl Call My Name* Chapters 18 - 23

Part I: Using Prior Knowledge and Contextual Clues
Below are the sentences in which the vocabulary words appear in the text. Read the sentence. Use any clues you can find in the sentence combined with your prior knowledge, and write what you think the underlined words mean in the space provided.

1. "Guess you might say I'm an agnostic."

2. On the second day there was another great feast and more dancing, and on the third morning the exodus began.

3 - 5. "When I try to put it into words, it comes out one of those unctuous, over-pious platitudes at which Bishops are expected to excel."

6. Already nothing looked the same because it was going to end, because he was going to leave it, and the thought filled him with a twinge of sudden anguish and the little, unexpected fear that precedes any big change, sad or joyous.

7. Here, where death waited behind each tree, he had made friends with loneliness, with death and deprivation, and, solidly against his back had stood the wall of his faith.

8. He had seen the sadness, the richness, the tragic poignancy of a way of life that each year, bit by bit, slipped beyond memory and was gone.

9. "You are the swimmer who came to us from the sea," and he put his arms around her and held her close, finding no words to say thank you for the sudden, unexpected gift of peace which they had offered him in their quiet, perceptive way.

10. "Say *please* and when she hands you the cup, say *thank you*. You'll find it most efficacious."

I Heard The Owl Vocabulary Chapters 18-23 Continued

Part II: Determining the Meaning - Match the vocabulary words to their dictionary definitions.

____ 35. agnostic
____ 36. exodus
____ 37. unctuous
____ 38. pious
____ 39. platitudes
____ 40. anguish
____ 41. deprivation
____ 42. poignancy
____ 43. perceptive
____ 44. efficacious

A. sentimental pretense of spirituality in speech or attitude; gushing
B. distress; extreme pain in body or mind
C. one who believes neither the existence or nature of God is known
D. effective; having the power to produce the intended effect
E. loss; to hinder from possessing
F. zealous in prayer or acts of worship; devout
G. discerning; intuitive judgment
H. trite, commonplace speech; dull or stale truisms
I. a going out
J. state of being piercingly effective or of being touched or moved

VOCABULARY ANSWER KEY
I Heard the Owl Call My Name

Chapters 1, 2, & 3
1. B
2. E
3. G
4. F
5. H
6. C
7. A
8. D

Chapters 4, 5, 6, & 7
9. E
10. F
11. D
12. C
13. A
14. G
15. H
16. B

Chapters 8, 9, 10, & 11
17. D
18. F
19. I
20. H
21. J
22. A
23. E
24. G
25. B
26. C

Chapters 12, 13, 14, 15, 16, & 17
27. E
28. F
29. B
30. D
31. G
32. A
33. H
34. C

Chapters 18, 19, 20, 21, 22, & 23
35. C
36. I
37. A
38. F
39. H
40. B
41. E
42. J
43. G
44. D

DAILY LESSONS

LESSON ONE

Objectives
1. To introduce the unit
2. To distribute books and other related materials
3. To help students understands what it means to be a missionary so they can better identify with the main character in the story

Activity #1

Invite a person who is/was a missionary to come and speak with your class. Have your speaker tell what it is like to be a missionary, tell some of his/her experiences, and explain what things are most important to having a successful mission. Be sure to allow time for questions and answers.

Activity #2

Distribute the materials for the unit: books, study guides, reading assignment sheets, etc. Explain to students how they should use these materials.

Study Guides Students should read the study guide questions for each reading assignment prior to beginning the reading assignment to get a feeling for what events and ideas are important in the section they are about to read. After reading the section, students will (as a class or individually) answer the questions to review the important events and ideas from that section of the book. Students should keep the study guides as study materials for the unit test.

Vocabulary Prior to reading a reading assignment, students will do vocabulary work related to the section of the book they are about to read. Following the completion of the reading of the book, there will be a vocabulary review of all the words used in the vocabulary assignments. Students should keep their vocabulary work as study materials for the unit test.

Reading Assignment Sheet You need to fill in the reading assignment sheet to let students know by when their reading has to be completed. You can either write the assignment sheet up on a side blackboard or bulletin board and leave it there for students to see each day, or you can "ditto" copies for each student to have. In either case, you should advise students to become very familiar with the reading assignments so they know what is expected of them.

Extra Activities Center The unit and vocabulary resource portions of this unit contains suggestions for an extra library of related books and articles in your classroom as well as crossword and word search puzzles. Make an extra activities center in your room where you will keep these materials for students to use. (Bring the books and articles in from the library and keep several copies of the puzzles on hand.) Explain to students that these materials are available for students to use when they finish reading assignments or other class work early.

<u>Nonfiction Assignment Sheet</u> Explain to students that they each are to read at least one non-fiction piece from the in-class library at some time during the unit. Students will fill out a nonfiction assignment sheet after completing the reading to help you evaluate their reading experiences and to help the students think about and evaluate their own reading experiences.

<u>Books</u> Each school has its own rules and regulations regarding student use of school books. Advise students of the procedures that are normal for your school.

NONFICTION ASSIGNMENT SHEET - *I Heard The Owl Call My Name*
(To be completed after reading the required nonfiction article)

Name _____ Date _____

Title of Nonfiction Read _____

Written By _____ Publication Date _____

I. Factual Summary: Write a short summary of the piece you read.

II. Vocabulary
    1. With which vocabulary words in the piece did you encounter some degree of difficulty?

    2. How did you resolve your lack of understanding with these words?

III. Interpretation: What was the main point the author wanted you to get from reading his work?

IV. Criticism
    1. With which points of the piece did you agree or find easy to accept? Why?

    2. With which points of the piece did you disagree or find difficult to believe? Why?

V. Personal Response: What do you think about this piece? <u>OR</u> How does this piece influence your ideas?

LESSON TWO

Objectives
1. To preview the study questions and vocabulary work for chapters 1-3
2. To read chapters 1-3
2. To begin the oral reading evaluations

Activity #1

Show students how to preview the study questions and do the prereading vocabulary worksheet for chapters 1-3. Give students time to complete the worksheet.

Activity #2

Have students chapters 1-3 orally in class. If your students have not had an oral reading evaluation this term, this would be a good chance to do one. A form is included in this unit for your convenience.

If students do not finish reading this assignment orally, they should complete it prior to the next class period.

LESSON THREE

Objectives
1. To review the main ideas and events from chapters 1-3
2. To preview the study questions and vocabulary for chapters 4-7
2. To read chapters 4-7
3. To continue the oral reading evaluations (if necessary)

Activity #1

Give students a few minutes to formulate answers for the study questions for chapters 1-3. Discuss students' answers in detail. Write the "correct" answers on the board for students to copy for study use.

Activity #2

Preview the study questions and have students do the vocabulary work for chapters 4-7 of *I Heard the Owl Call My Name*.

Activity #3

Have students read chapters 4-7. If you are doing oral reading evaluations and need this class period to continue the evaluations, have students read orally. Otherwise, have students read silently.

If students do not complete reading this assignment in class, they should do so prior to the next class meeting.

ORAL READING EVALUATION - *I Heard The Owl Call My Name*

Name _____ Class _____ Date _____

SKILL	EXCELLENT	GOOD	AVERAGE	FAIR	POOR
Fluency	5	4	3	2	1
Clarity	5	4	3	2	1
Audibility	5	4	3	2	1
Pronunciation	5	4	3	2	1
_____	5	4	3	2	1
_____	5	4	3	2	1

Total _____ Grade _____

Comments:

LESSON FOUR

Objectives
1. To review the main ideas and events from chapters 4-7
2. To preview the study questions for chapters 8-11
4. To familiarize students with the vocabulary in chapters 8-11
5. To read chapters 8-11
6. To give students the opportunity to practice writing their personal opinions
7. To give the teacher the opportunity to evaluate students' writing skills
8. To get students to think about one idea presented by the book

Activity #1
Quiz - Distribute quizzes and give students about 10 minutes to complete them. (Note: The quizzes may either be the short answer study guides or the multiple choice version for chapters 4-7.) Have students exchange papers. Grade the quizzes as a class. Collect the papers for recording the grades. (If you used the multiple choice version as a quiz, take a few minutes to discuss the answers for the short answer version if your students are using the short answer version for their study guides.)

Activity #2
Tell students that prior to your next class meeting they should do the prereading and reading work for chapters 8-11.

Activity #3
Distribute Writing Assignment #1. Discuss the directions in detail and give students ample time to complete the assignment.

WRITING ASSIGNMENT #1 - *I Heard the Owl Call My Name*

PROMPT

To become a part of a group, you need to have something in common with the group. Usually the one trying to join the group begins acting more like the people in the group he/she wishes to join. For example, if you want to be a member of the band, you need to play an instrument. If you want to be a member of the soccer team, you need to know how to play soccer. If you want to be part of the popular group of kids at school, you need to do whatever they do -- and so on.

Mark wanted to fulfill his duties as vicar at Kingcome. In order to do that, he had to have the trust of the Indian people. To get their trust and to be able to do his job, he worked hard at learning the Indian ways and language. He was a minority (white, Anglo) trying to fit in with the dominant (Indian) culture.

The United States has long been known as the "melting pot" -- a place where people of many different heritages blend into one country. People from all over the world gave up their own cultures and languages to make a new nation. French, Germans, Italians, Spanish, Chinese, Africans, Vietnamese, Koreans -- people from almost every nation and culture on Earth have become American citizens over the years.

Each population group has retained pride in its roots; just look at the number of ethnic festivals held around our country each year to see that. Some minority cultures believe they should maintain all of their cultural heritage as well as their own languages. The "white men" understood that the tribes of North American Indians wanted to maintain their own ways of life and have nothing to do with the "white man's" culture; thus, reservations were set up. That was a relatively easy solution at the time it was done. Today, however, there aren't any new lands to or set aside for various ethnic groups who wish to maintain their individualism.

Good or bad, right or wrong, healthy for our country or not, the issues of minority rights are heatedly debated, and the interest in cultural individuality versus the traditional "melting pot" is a growing factor.

Your assignment is to write a composition in which you give your own opinions about some aspect of these kinds of minority/assimilation issues.

PREWRITING

Stop and think for a minute. Is there any minority culture issue that you have a particular interest in or opinion about? If so, you've found your topic. If not, tell what you think about the whole cultural individuality versus melting pot issue.

Jot down your ideas, your thoughts. Organize your thoughts into some logical sequence.

DRAFTING

The format for this composition is not very rigid. Just make sure you have an introductory paragraph, that your paragraphs in the body of your composition have and follow topic sentences, and that you have a concluding paragraph to wrap up your thoughts.

PROOFREADING

When you finish the rough draft of your paper, ask a student who sits near you to read it. After reading your rough draft, he/she should tell you what he/she liked best about your work, which parts were difficult to understand, and ways in which your work could be improved. Reread your paper considering your critic's comments, and make the corrections you think are necessary.

LESSON FIVE

Objectives
1. To review the main ideas and events from chapters 8-11
2. To preview the study questions and vocabulary for chapters 12-17
3. To make the nonfiction reading assignment
4. To give students the opportunity to gather information for the nonfiction assignment
5. To increase students' awareness about the Indians of North America

Activity #1
Give students a few minutes to preview the study questions for chapters 8-11. Discuss students' answers in detail. Make sure students have the "correct" answers from which to study.

Activity #2
Tell students to complete the prereading and reading work for chapters 12-17 of *I Heard the Owl Call My Name* prior to your next class meeting.

Activity #3
Take your class to your library/media center.

Divide your class into three groups:
- Group I - Indian tribes of Western North America
- Group II - Current affairs relating to Indians of Western North America
- Group III - Animals in the Indian cultures (significance of Owl, Salmon, Eagle, etc.)

Each group should meet briefly to discuss how they will tackle their topic and to decide what each group member should research. Then, the group members should use the library/media center to find the appropriate information.

LESSON SIX

Objectives
1. To review the main ideas and events of chapters 12-17
2. To preview the study questions and vocabulary for chapters 18-23
3. To read chapters 18-23

Activity #1
Give students a few minutes to formulate answers to the study questions for chapters 12-17. Discuss students' answers. Make sure students have the correct answers from which to study.

Activity #2
Give students the remainder of this class period to preview the study questions, do the related vocabulary worksheet, and read chapters 18-23. If students do not complete this in class, they should do so prior to your next class meeting.

LESSON SEVEN

Objectives
1. To review the main events and ideas from chapters 18-23
2. To discuss the novel on interpretive and critical levels

Activity #1
Use the study questions as a short quiz to check to see that students did the reading assignment and to check their understanding of the assignment. Discuss the answers to the quiz in detail.

Activity #2
Choose the questions from the Extra Discussion Questions/Writing Assignments which seem most appropriate for your students. A class discussion of these questions is most effective if students have been given the opportunity to formulate answers to the questions prior to the discussion. To this end, you may either have all the students formulate answers to all the questions, divide your class into groups and assign one or more questions to each group, or you could assign one question to each student in your class. The option you choose will make a difference in the amount of class time needed for this activity.

Activity #3
After students have had ample time to formulate answers to the questions, begin your class discussion of the questions and the ideas presented by the questions. Be sure students take notes during the discussion so they have information to study for the unit test.

EXTRA DISCUSSION QUESTIONS - *I Heard the Owl Call My Name*

Interpretation
1. What are the conflicts in the story and how are they resolved?
2. What is the setting of the story, and how important is the setting to the story? If it were set in another place and time, would the story have been as effective?
3. Where is the climax of the story? Defend your choice.
4. Are the characters in *I Heard the Owl Call My Name* stereotypes? If so, explain the usefulness of employing stereotypes in the novel. If they are not, explain how they merit individuality.
5. What is Mark's job as vicar? What is the point of his being at Kingcome?
6. In what ways was modern (western) culture invading the traditional culture of the Indians in he novel? Why was modern (western) culture invading the traditional Indian culture?
7. Explain the use of the Victorian "we" and why Mark decided to stop using it.
8. From what point of view is the story written, and how does that affect our attitudes as we read?

Critical
9. Explain the significance of the title of *I Heard the Owl Call My Name*.
10. Explain the comparison of man to the salmon and, more specifically, Mark's life to the "swimmer."
11. Of what was the mask a symbol? Explain your answer fully.
12. Compare and contrast Mark and the RCMP officer.
13. Compare and contrast Keetah and her sister.
14. Compare and contrast Gordon and Jim.

Critical/Personal Response
15. Is the story of *I Heard the Owl Call My Name* believable? Explain why or why not.
16. What messages are presented to the readers of this book?
17. What is "civilization"? Explain how that word relates to this novel.
18. The interracial marriage between Mrs. Hudson's granddaughter and the white man did not work. Why do you suppose it did not work? What problems could have surfaced? What problems, if any, face interracial marriages today?

Personal Response
19. Does society have a right or a need to impose its culture on the subcultures within that society? Why or why not? Is society's culture imposed, or is it an event that just happens naturally?
20. Did you enjoy reading *I Heard the Owl Call My Name*? Why or why not?
21. Have you read any other books about missionaries or Indian cultures? What were they, and how did they compare to *I Heard the Owl Call My Name*?

LESSON EIGHT

Objective
   To review all of the vocabulary work done in this unit

Activity
   Choose one (or more) of the vocabulary review activities listed on the next page(s) and spend your class period as directed in the activity. Some of the materials for these review activities are located in the Vocabulary Resource Section of this unit.

VOCABULARY REVIEW ACTIVITIES

1. Divide your class into two teams and have an old-fashioned spelling or definition bee.

2. Give each of your students (or students in groups of two, three or four) an *I Heard the Owl Call My Name* Vocabulary Word Search Puzzle. The person (group) to find all of the vocabulary words in the puzzle first wins.

3. Give students an *I Heard the Owl Call My Name* Vocabulary Word Search Puzzle without the word list. The person or group to find the most vocabulary words in the puzzle wins.

4. Use an *I Heard the Owl Call My Name* Vocabulary Crossword Puzzle. Put the puzzle onto a transparency on the overhead projector (so everyone can see it), and do the puzzle together as a class.

5. Give students an *I Heard the Owl Call My Name* Vocabulary Matching Worksheet to do.

6. Divide your class into two teams. Use *I Heard the Owl Call My Name* vocabulary words with their letters jumbled as a word list. Student 1 from Team A faces off against Student 1 from Team B. You write the first jumbled word on the board. The first student (1A or 1B) to unscramble the word wins the chance for his/her team to score points. If 1A wins the jumble, go to student 2A and give him/her a definition. He/she must give you the correct spelling of the vocabulary word which fits that definition. If he/she does, Team A scores a point, and you give student 3A a definition for which you expect a correctly spelled matching vocabulary word. Continue giving Team A definitions until some team member makes an incorrect response. An incorrect response sends the game back to the jumbled-word face off, this time with students 2A and 2B. Instead of repeating giving definitions to the first few students of each team, continue with the student after the one who gave the last incorrect response on the team. For example, if Team B wins the jumbled-word face-off, and student 5B gave the last incorrect answer for Team B, you would start this round of definition questions with student 6B, and so on. The team with the most points wins!

7. Have students write a story in which they correctly use as many vocabulary words as possible. Have students read their compositions orally! Post the most original compositions on your bulletin board!

LESSON NINE

Objective

    To give students time to work on their research assignments

Activity

    Give students the first part of this class period to finish gathering and reading their research information (from Lesson Five). In the second half of the class time, students should get together in their small groups to discuss the articles/information they have found.

LESSON TEN

Objectives

    1. To prepare students for their nonfiction reading reports
    2. To give students the opportunity to practice writing to inform
    3. To give the teacher the opportunity to evaluate students' writing skills

Activity

    Distribute Writing Assignment #2. Discuss the directions in detail and give students ample time to complete the assignment.

LESSONS ELEVEN AND TWELVE

Objectives

    1. To give students the opportunity to practice public speaking
    2. To expose all students to a wealth of information about Western North American Indians and Indian cultures

Activity

    Have each student give an oral report about the specific topic he/she researched. Begin with students who researched Western North American Indian tribes. Have each student in that group report. Follow that with students from the Animals in Indian cultures group. Finally, have students from the Current Affairs group give their reports. Use these reports as springboards for related discussions.

WRITING ASSIGNMENT #2 - *I Heard the Owl Call My Name*

PROMPT
You have gathered information about your topic, and in a few days you will have to give an oral presentation about that information. The purpose of this assignment is to help you prepare for that presentation. Your assignment is to write a composition in which you explain what you plan to say in your presentation.

PREWRITING
Review the notes you took as you were reading the article(s) you found. Jot down the main categories of information or main points you want to make in your presentation. Make a little outline in which you organize the categories/main points into a logical order.

DRAFTING
Write a paragraph in which you introduce your topic.

In the body of your composition write a paragraph for each main category/main point you wish to make. Fill in each paragraph with details and information about the main category/main point.

Write a paragraph in which you conclude your report.

PROMPT
When you finish the rough draft of your composition, ask a student from your group to read it. After reading your rough draft, he/she should tell you what he/she liked best about your work, which parts were difficult to understand, and ways in which your work could be improved. Reread your paper considering your critic's comments, and make the corrections you think are necessary.

PROOFREADING
Do a final proofreading of your paper double-checking your grammar, spelling, organization, and the clarity of your ideas.

ORAL REPORT EVALUATION - *I Heard The Owl Call My Name*

Name _____ Topic _____

Class _____ Date _____ Grade _____

SKILL	EXCELLENT	GOOD	AVERAGE	FAIR	POOR
Posture	5	4	3	2	1
Clarity of Content	5	4	3	2	1
Audibility	5	4	3	2	1
Eye Contact	5	4	3	2	1
Enthusiasm	5	4	3	2	1
_____	5	4	3	2	1

Total _____

Strengths:

Weaknesses:

Comments:

LESSON THIRTEEN

Objective
    To discuss the positive and negative aspects of living in a multicultural society

Activity
    Read several students' Writing Assignment #1s and use them as springboards for discussions about living in a multicultural society. You will probably have many different ideas and viewpoints presented in the writing assignments, which will give a good base for reactions and discussions.

LESSON FOURTEEN

Objectives
    1. To give students the opportunity to practice writing to persuade
    2. To get students to think about some current issues relating to minority rights
    3. To give the teacher the opportunity to evaluate students' writing skills

Activity #1
    Distribute Writing Assignment #3. Discuss the directions in detail and give students ample time to complete the assignment.

Activity #2
    While students are working on the writing assignment, call individual students to your desk or some other private area to discuss their first two writing assignments. An evaluation form is enclosed for your convenience.

LESSON FIFTEEN

Objective
    To review the main ideas presented in *I Heard the Owl Call My Name*

Activity #1
    Choose one of the review games/activities included in the packet and spend your class period as outlined there. Some materials for these activities are located in the Extra Activities Packet section of this unit.

Activity #2
    Remind students that the Unit Test will be in the next class meeting. Stress the review of the Study Guides and their class notes as a last minute, brush-up review for homework.

WRITING EVALUATION FORM - *I Heard the Owl Call My Name*

Name _____ Date _____

Grade _____

Circle One For Each Item:

Grammar:	correct	errors noted on paper
Spelling:	correct	errors noted on paper
Punctuation:	correct	errors noted on paper
Legibility:	excellent	good fair poor
Communication of Idea:	excellent	good fair poor

Strengths:

Weaknesses:

Comments/Suggestions:

WRITING ASSIGNMENT #3 - *I Heard the Owl Call My Name*

PROMPT

We have discussed many issues relating to minority subcultures within a larger culture. One issue that has been heatedly debated in our country is whether or not minority cultures should be allowed to keep their own languages, especially in cities and states where there is a large concentration of a particular minority group.

Your assignment is to write a persuasive letter to your congressman either persuading him or her that areas heavily populated by a minority culture should or should not use that minority group's language as the predominant language in that area. (Predominant language would mean that all street signs and other signs in public places would be in that language, that language would be used in the school system with English taught as a second language, etc.)

PREWRITING

On one side of a scratch sheet of paper, write down all the reasons why a large population of a minority culture should be allowed to have its own language as the predominant language in its area. On the other side of the paper, jot down reasons why a minority culture should not be allowed to have its own language as the predominant language in its area.

Considering the reasons on both sides of the page, decide on which side of the issue you fall. Do you think they should or should not?

DRAFTING

Use a business letter format.

Write a paragraph in which you introduce your topic and state your position on the issue.

In the body of your letter, write one paragraph for each of the reasons why minority cultures should (or should not) be allowed to have their own languages as the predominant language in the areas where large populations of the group live. State your reason in the topic sentence and give specific examples to fill out the paragraph.

Write a concluding paragraph in which you summarize your main points and thank your representative for his/her time and consideration of your opinions.

PROMPT

When you finish the rough draft of your paper, ask a student who sits near you to read it. After reading your rough draft, he/she should tell you what he/she liked best about your work, which parts were difficult to understand, and ways in which your work could be improved. Reread your paper considering your critic's comments, and make the corrections you think are necessary.

PROOFREADING

Do a final proofreading of your paper double-checking your grammar, spelling, organization, and the clarity of your ideas.

REVIEW GAMES/ACTIVITIES - *I Heard the Owl Call My Name*

1. Ask the class to make up a unit test for *I Heard the Owl Call My Name*. The test should have 4 sections: matching, true/false, short answer, and essay. Students may use 1/2 period to make the test and then swap papers and use the other 1/2 class period to take a test a classmate has devised. (open book) You may want to use the unit test included in this packet or take questions from the students' unit tests to formulate your own test.

2. Take 1/2 period for students to make up true and false questions (including the answers). Collect the papers and divide the class into two teams. Draw a big tic-tac-toe board on the chalk board. Make one team X and one team O. Ask questions to each side, giving each student one turn. If the question is answered correctly, that students' team's letter (X or O) is placed in the box. If the answer is incorrect, no mark is placed in the box. The object is to get three marks in a row like tic-tac-toe. You may want to keep track of the number of games won for each team.

3. Take 1/2 period for students to make up questions (true/false and short answer). Collect the questions. Divide the class into two teams. You'll alternate asking questions to individual members of teams A & B (like in a spelling bee). The question keeps going from A to B until it is correctly answered, then a new question is asked. A correct answer does not allow the team to get another question. Correct answers are +2 points; incorrect answers are -1 point.

4. Have students pair up and quiz each other from their study guides and class notes.

5. Give students an *I Heard the Owl Call My Name* crossword puzzle to complete.

6. Divide your class into two teams. Use *I Heard the Owl Call My Name* crossword words with their letters jumbled as a word list. Student 1 from Team A faces off against Student 1 from Team B. You write the first jumbled word on the board. The first student (1A or 1B) to unscramble the word wins the chance for his/her team to score points. If 1A wins the jumble, go to student 2A and give him/her a clue. He/she must give you the correct word which matches that clue. If he/she does, Team A scores a point, and you give student 3A a clue for which you expect another correct response. Continue giving Team A clues until some team member makes an incorrect response. An incorrect response sends the game back to the jumbled-word face off, this time with students 2A and 2B. Instead of repeating giving clues to the first few students of each team, continue with the student after the one who gave the last incorrect response on the team. For example, if Team B wins the jumbled-word face-off, and student 5B gave the last incorrect answer for Team B, you would start this round of clue questions with student 6B, and so on. The team with the most points wins!

UNIT TESTS

SHORT ANSWER UNIT TEST #1 - *I Heard the Owl Call My Name*

I. Matching/Identify

___ 1. Calamity Bill   A. Chief

___ 2. Bishop   B. Retired canon; helps Mark get started

___ 3. Caleb   C. Village matriarch

___ 4. Jim   D. Goes with Gordon but returns to Jim

___ 5. T. P.   E. Adopts white man's ways & ambitions

___ 6. Eddy   F. Mark scatters his ashes

___ 7. Mrs. Hudson   G. Vicar

___ 8. Keetah   H. Village

___ 9. Peter   I. Takes Mark to Kingcome & becomes his friend

___ 10. Gordon   J. The carver

___ 11. Kingcome   K. Sends Mark to Kingcome

___ 12. Mark   L. Elder of the tribe

Owl Short Answer Unit Test 1 Page 2

II. Short Answer
1. What information does the Preface reveal?

2. What is a potlatch?

3. Why has it taken so long for the RCMP officer to come and issue the burial permit?

4. Identify: "He will say we and he will mean us."

5. What does Mark mean when he says the death of the swimmer is a triumph?

6. What is the "strange little wind of dissent" that Mark feels?

I Heard the Owl Call My Name Short Answer Unit Test 1 Page 3

7. Why does Mrs. Hudson say to Mark, "What have you done to us?"

8. What happened to Keetah's sister?

9. Describe the visitors who come to the village.

10. What gift do the villagers offer Mark?

I Heard the Owl Call My Name Short Answer Unit Test 1 Page 4

III. Essay

What are we to learn from reading *I Heard the Owl Call My Name*?

IV. Vocabulary

Listen to the vocabulary words and write them down. Go back later and fill in the definitions.

1.

2.

3.

4.

5.

6.

7.

8.

9.

10.

KEY: SHORT ANSWER UNIT TEST #1 - *I Heard the Owl Call My Name*

I. Matching/Identify

F	1. Calamity Bill	A. Chief
K	2. Bishop	B. Retired canon; helps Mark get started
B	3. Caleb	C. Village matriarch
I	4. Jim	D. Goes with Gordon but returns to Jim
L	5. T.P.	E. Adopts white man's ways & ambitions
A	6. Eddy	F. Mark scatters his ashes
C	7. Mrs. Hudson	G. Vicar
D	8. Keetah	H. Village
J	9. Peter	I. Takes Mark to Kingcome & becomes his friend
E	10. Gordon	J. The carver
H	11. Kingcome	K. Sends Mark to Kingcome
G	12. Mark	L. Elder of the tribe

II. Short Answer

1. What information does the Preface reveal?
    The young ordained has only a few years to live and he will spend them serving Indian villages. The Bishop describes Kingcome as his hardest parish, yet it is where he would go if he were in the young man's place.

2. What is a potlatch?
    It is a feast with gifts given by the leader of one Indian tribe to another tribe in order to impress his wealth and status upon the neighboring tribe.

3. Why has it taken so long for the RCMP officer to come and issue the burial permit?
    Evidently, he has waited for a fair day so that he could bring his girlfriend.

4. Identify: "He will say we and he will mean us."
    Jim is discussing Mark with Chief Eddy. He is referring to Mark's use of the Victorian "we" in asking Jim what needs to be done. It appears that the Indians are familiar with people using the word "we" when they want the Indians to do something for them.

5. What does Mark mean when he says the death of the swimmer is a triumph?
    He means that the salmon has lived its life and exhausted its energy completely for the purpose it was created. It has returned to spawn and die as God intended. Its life is a success, not a sadness.

6. What is the "strange little wind of dissent" that Mark feels?
    It is the tension between the old ways and traditions of the elders and the new "outside world" ways the children bring back to the village from school.

7. Why does Mrs. Hudson say to Mark, "What have you done to us?"
    She is speaking to Mark, the white man, not Mark the vicar who is becoming a part of the village life. Mrs. Hudson's granddaughter returned to the village in the clothes and make-up of the white world, and with her white man, she practically stole a part of the villagers' pride and heritage. Mrs. Hudson is taking out her frustrations about the new ways taking over the old.

8. What happened to Keetah's sister?
    The white man deserted her in Vancouver, where she died within three months. The world of a town was completely alien to her, and her only course of survival was to prostitute herself and bury her shame and despair in alcohol and drugs.

9. Describe the visitors who come to the village.
    The California group questioned Mark about the villagers as though they were merely interesting objects for their entertainment. The English woman had studied their culture, yet still only saw the Indians as objects of her study. Neither saw the Indians as being human.

10. What gift do the villagers offer Mark?
    They offer him a place to die in peace with friends and family; they ask him to remain with them.

III. Essay
    What are we to learn from reading *I Heard the Owl Call My Name*?

IV. Vocabulary
    Choose ten words from the vocabulary lists. Read the words orally and have the students write them down. Tell students to go back later and fill in the definitions.

SHORT ANSWER UNIT TEST 2 - *I Heard the Owl Call My Name*

I. Matching/Identify

___ 1. Calamity Bill   A. Vicar

___ 2. Bishop   B. Elder of the tribe

___ 3. Caleb   C. The carver

___ 4. Jim   D. Mark scatters his ashes

___ 5. T. P.   E. Sends Mark to Kingcome

___ 6. Eddy   F. Goes with Gordon but returns to Jim

___ 7. Mrs. Hudson   G. Chief

___ 8. Keetah   H. Village

___ 9. Peter   I. Takes Mark to Kingcome & becomes his friend

___ 10. Gordon   J. Village matriarch

___ 11. Kingcome   K. Adopts white man's ways & ambitions

___ 12. Mark   L. Retired canon; helps Mark get started

I Heard the Owl Call My Name Short Answer Unit Test 2 Page 2

II. Short Answer

1. Before Mark meets the Indians, how does he think they will respond to him? Why?

2. Identify: "If man were to vanish from this planet tomorrow, here he would leave no trace that he ever was."

3. What does it tell us about Mark that he "sensed there was something yet unfinished of which he had no part"?

4. What are the two kinds of naivete Mark quotes from Schweitzer?

5. Why do you think "the watchful waiting left the Indian's eyes"?

6. What does Mark mean when he says the death of the swimmer is a triumph?

7. Why does Mrs. Hudson say to Mark, "What have you done to us?"

I Heard the Owl Call My Name Short Answer Unit Test 2 Page 3

8. What happened to Keetah's sister?

9. Describe the visitors who come to the village.

10. What do the old people of the village fear in Gordon?

11. Why does Keetah return?

12. Why do you think the Bishop feels that it's "easier here, where only the fundamentals count, to learn . . . enough of the meaning of life to be ready to die"?

13. Why did Mark say to Marta, "On the bank of the river I heard the owl call my name"?

14. How is Mark's death, like the swimmer's, a triumph?

I Heard the Owl Call My Name Short Answer Unit Test 2 Page 4

III. Composition

The Dell paperback edition of *I Heard the Owl Call My Name* says, "Here, in a remote tribal enclave, he [Mark] will experience the meaning of faith, courage, dignity, and patience. here, in a world of simple truths and profound silences, he will learn how to live. And how to die." Explain specifically how this statement relates to the book.

IV. Vocabulary

Listen to the vocabulary words and write them down. Go back later and fill in the definitions.

1.

2.

3.

4.

5.

6.

7.

8.

9.

10.

KEY: SHORT ANSWER UNIT TEST 2 - *I Heard the Owl Call My Name*

I. Matching/Identify

D	1. Calamity Bill	A.	Vicar
E	2. Bishop	B.	Elder of the tribe
L	3. Caleb	C.	The carver
I	4. Jim	D.	Mark scatters his ashes
B	5. T. P.	E.	Sends Mark to Kingcome
G	6. Eddy	F.	Goes with Gordon but returns to Jim
J	7. Mrs. Hudson	G.	Chief
F	8. Keetah	H.	Village
C	9. Peter	I.	Takes Mark to Kingcome & becomes his friend
K	10. Gordon	J.	Village matriarch
H	11. Kingcome	K.	Adopts white man's ways & ambitions
A	12. Mark	L.	Retired canon; helps Mark get started

II. Short Answer

1. Before Mark meets the Indians, how does he think they will respond to him? Why?
   He thinks they will respond to him with arrogance because he has heard of their intelligence and their lavish feasts where gifts are distributed to all guests by the host chief who wishes to impress upon them his great wealth.

2. Identify the speaker: "If man were to vanish from this planet tomorrow, here he would leave no trace that he ever was."
   Mark was describing the awesome grandeur and beauty of the British Columbian coast.

3. What does it tell us about Mark that he "sensed there was something yet unfinished of which he had no part"?

   It illustrates his respect and consideration for the traditions and values of the Indians.

4. What are the two kinds of naivete Mark quotes from Schweitzer?

   One kind of naivete is not even being aware that there exists a problem or situation. The other kind is the naivete of a man who has searched for answers and discovered that man knows little, yet he retains his convictions and beliefs.

5. Why do you think "the watchful waiting left the Indian's eyes"?

   Mark quoted an old Indian prayer that Jim had forgotten. This made Jim take an interest in Mark as more than just the new vicar who must be accommodated. Jim looks at Mark as another man and potential friend after this exchange because Mark has shown his real interest in the people and their ways.

6. What does Mark mean when he says the death of the swimmer is a triumph?

   He means that the salmon has lived its life and exhausted its energy completely for the purpose it was created. It has returned to spawn and die as God intended. Its life is a success, not a sadness.

7. Why does Mrs. Hudson say to Mark, "What have you done to us?"

   She is speaking to Mark, the white man, not Mark the vicar who is becoming a part of the village life. Mrs. Hudson's granddaughter returned to the village in the clothes and make-up of the white world, and with her white man, she practically stole a part of the villagers' pride and heritage. Mrs. Hudson is taking out her frustrations about the new ways taking over the old.

8. What happened to Keetah's sister?

   The white man deserted her in Vancouver, where she died within three months. The world of a town was completely alien to her, and her only course of survival was to prostitute herself and bury her shame and despair in alcohol and drugs.

9. Describe the visitors who come to the village.

   The California group questioned Mark about the villagers as though they were merely interesting objects for their entertainment. The English woman had studied their culture, yet still only saw the Indians as objects of her study. Neither saw the Indians as being human.

10. What do the old people of the village fear in Gordon?

    They fear his desire to become an educated and professional man and therefore not a part of the village community. They are afraid of the end of their identity as a people. They are afraid that their village is dying.

11. Why does Keetah return?

    She cannot adjust to the white man's world; she has known and loved her village ways for too long. She realizes that although Gordon has become very "white," she will always remain an Indian.

12. Why do you think the Bishop feels that it's "easier here, where only the fundamentals count, to learn . . . enough of the meaning of life to be ready to die"?

    Although life is primitive in the villages, it encompasses all the human needs: love, work, play, death, hope, etc. The struggles of human life are clearer in this setting, as are the achievements.

13. Why did Mark say to Marta, "On the bank of the river I heard the owl call my name"?

    He senses he is seriously ill and dying and wants to know if it is true.

14. How is Mark's death, like the swimmer's, a triumph?

    He lived a short yet full, rich life. Like the swimmer, he died in a triumph of achievement. His purpose was fulfilled.

III. Composition

   The Dell paperback edition of *I Heard the Owl Call My Name* says, "Here, in a remote tribal enclave, he [Mark] will experience the meaning of faith, courage, dignity, and patience. here, in a world of simple truths and profound silences, he will learn how to live. And how to die." Explain specifically how this statement relates to the book.

IV. Vocabulary

   Choose ten words from the vocabulary lists. Read the words orally and have the students write them down. Tell students to go back later and fill in the definitions.

ADVANCED SHORT ANSWER UNIT TEST - *I Heard the Owl Call My Name*

I. Matching
I. Matching/Identify

___ 1. Calamity Bill   A. Vicar

___ 2. Bishop   B. Elder of the tribe

___ 3. Caleb   C. The carver

___ 4. Jim   D. Mark scatters his ashes

___ 5. T. P.   E. Sends Mark to Kingcome

___ 6. Eddy   F. Goes with Gordon but returns to Jim

___ 7. Mrs. Hudson   G. Chief

___ 8. Keetah   H. Village

___ 9. Peter   I. Takes Mark to Kingcome & becomes his friend

___ 10. Gordon   J. Village matriarch

___ 11. Kingcome   K. Adopts white man's ways & ambitions

___ 12. Mark   L. Retired canon; helps Mark get started

I Heard the Owl Call My Name Advanced Short Answer Unit Test Page 2

II. Short Answer

1. What is Mark's job as vicar? What is the point of his being at Kingcome?

2. In what ways was modern (western) culture invading the traditional culture of the Indians in the novel? Why was modern (western) culture invading the traditional Indian culture?

3. Explain the comparison of man to the salmon and, more specifically, Mark's life to the "swimmer."

4. Of what was the mask a symbol? Explain your answer fully.

5. Compare and contrast Mark and the RCMP officer.

6. Compare and contrast Keetah and her sister.

I Heard the Owl Call My Name Advanced Short Answer Unit Test Page 3

7. Compare and contrast Gordon and Jim.

8. What does it tell us about Mark that he "sensed there was something yet unfinished of which he had no part"?

9. Why does Mrs. Hudson say to Mark, "What have you done to us?"

10. Why do you think the Bishop feels that it's "easier here, where only the fundamentals count, to learn . . . enough of the meaning of life to be ready to die"?

I Heard the Owl Call My Name Advanced Short Answer Unit Test Page 4

III. Composition

"Past the village flowed the river, like time, like life itself, waiting for the swimmer to come again on his way to the climax of his adventurous life, and to the end for which he had been made."

Explain why this paragraph is an appropriate ending paragraph for the book *I Heard the Owl Call My Name*.

I Heard the Owl Call My Name Advanced Short Answer Unit Test Page 5

III. Vocabulary

    Listen to the vocabulary words and write them down. Later go back and write a story using all of the vocabulary words.

MULTIPLE CHOICE UNIT TEST #1 - *I Heard the Owl Call My Name*

I. Matching/Identify

___ 1. Calamity Bill   A. Chief

___ 2. Bishop   B. Retired canon; helps Mark get started

___ 3. Caleb   C. Village matriarch

___ 4. Jim   D. Goes with Gordon but returns to Jim

___ 5. T. P.   E. Adopts white man's ways & ambitions

___ 6. Eddy   F. Mark scatters his ashes

___ 7. Mrs. Hudson   G. Vicar

___ 8. Keetah   H. Village

___ 9. Peter   I. Takes Mark to Kingcome & becomes his friend

___ 10. Gordon   J. The carver

___ 11. Kingcome   K. Sends Mark to Kingcome

___ 12. Mark   L. Elder of the tribe

II. Multiple Choice

1. What information does the preface reveal?
     a. It explains the Indian culture.
     b. It tells about the priest's life before he came to the village.
     c. It tells about the young vicar's illness.
     d. It tells why the author wrote the book.

2. Before Mark meets the Indians, how does he think they will respond to him?
     a. He thinks they will be arrogant.
     b. He thinks they will be wary and unfriendly.
     c. He thinks they will be cautious but congenial.
     d. He thinks they will be very friendly.

I Heard the Owl Call My Name Multiple Choice Unit Test 1 Page 2

3. Identify the speaker: "If man were to vanish from this planet tomorrow, here he would leave no trace that he ever was."
    a. It was the bishop.
    b. It was Caleb.
    c. It was Jim.
    d. It was Mark.

4. What does it tell us about Mark that he "sensed there was something yet unfinished of which he had no part?"
    a. It illustrates his respect and consideration for the traditions and values of the Indians.
    b. It shows that he is a very fearful, almost paranoid, person.
    c. It shows that he does not make friends easily.
    d. It shows that he is a procrastinator; he has trouble completing a task.

5. What advice does the Bishop write to Mark?
    a. The bishop suggests Mark must work with his hands to gain the respect of the Indians.
    b. He tells Mark to hire some white men to help with the project.
    c. He tells Mark to let the Indians do all of the work.
    d. He suggests that Mark leave everything the way it is for at least six months, until the Indians are used to him.

6. What word is missing in this statement of Mark's? "One kind of_____ is not even being aware that a problem exists. The other kind is the _____ of a man who has searched for answers and discovered that man knows little, yet he retains his convictions and beliefs."
    a. Selfishness
    b. Question
    c. Naivete
    d. Sin

7. What happened when Mark quoted an old Indian prayer that Jim had forgotten?
    a. Jim got upset and told Mark never to speak the holy words of the Indians.
    b. Jim accepted him as a potential friend because of Mark's interest in the people.
    c. Jim got a frightened look on his face and ran away.
    d. Jim was insulted and embarrassed.

8. What does Jim mean when he calls Gordon "fast moving water" and Keetah "the pool?"
    a. He thinks they will be a good match for each other.
    b. He thinks they are not well suited for each other.
    c. These are Gordon and Keetah's other Indian names.
    d. These are the roles Gordon and Keetah have in a tribal ritual.

I Heard the Owl Call My Name Multiple Choice Unit Test 1 Page 3

9. What is the "strange little wind of dissent" that Mark feels?
    a. A winter blizzard is approaching.
    b. It is the tension between the old ways and the new.
    c. He thinks the Bishop is displeased with his work.
    d. He had a disagreement with Jim and is worried that their friendship is in jeopardy.

10. Why is Mrs. Hudson's family leaving the village in shame?
    a. Her granddaughter and the white man are living together before they are married, and this is not permitted.
    b. Her granddaughter and the white man have bought the valuable mask from Gordon's uncle after getting him drunk.
    c. The white man has ridiculed the Indians' customs and refused to have any of them at his wedding.
    d. The white man is a gambler and the Indians do not play cards. They think it is evil.

11. True or False: When Mrs. Hudson talks to Mark and says "What have you done to us?" she is blaming him for her misfortune.
    a. True
    b. False

12. Which statement describes the visitors who come to the village?
    a. They were interested primarily in the Indians as human beings.
    b. They were interested in the Indians as objects of study and amusement, not as people.
    c. They were tourists just interested in finding a good fishing spot.
    d. They were desperate for food and shelter.

13. How do the old people of the village feel about Gordon?
    a. They accept him for who he is.
    b. They are jealous of him.
    c. They fear him and his ideas.
    d. They are not particularly concerned. They think he is a foolish young man who will come to his senses.

14. Marta writes to the Bishop and tells him she is "keeping her promise now." What is her promise?
    a. She has agreed to stay at the vicarage until she retires.
    b. She has trained the young village girls to be good housewives.
    c. She has notified the Bishop that Mark's health is failing.
    d. She has converted to Christianity.

I Heard the Owl Call My Name Multiple Choice Unit Test 1 Page 4

15. What does the Bishop think about life in the villages?
    a. He thinks village life is much more difficult than life elsewhere because of the lack of conveniences.
    b. He thinks the struggles and achievements of life are clearer in the village.
    c. He dismisses it without much thought.
    d. He wonders if anyone there will ever be converted to Christianity.

16. Why did Mark say to Marta, "On the bank of the river I heard the owl call my name?"
    a. He was delirious with a fever and didn't know what he was talking about.
    b. He was explaining that he finally felt accepted into the village.
    c. He sensed that he was dying and wanted to know if it were true.
    d. He was talking symbolically about the blending of the old customs and the modern way of life. He felt like he was the bridge between the two.

17. Which of the following statements describes Mark's life/death?
    a. He lived a short yet full, rich life. He died in a triumph of achievement like the swimmer.
    b. He lived only through others, like the reflection on the water.
    c. His life was hollow, like the wind.
    d. His death was sudden, like a flame being extinguished.

I Heard the Owl Call My Name Multiple Choice Test 1 Page 5

III. Composition

> Explain how and why Mark assimilated into the Indian culture in Kingcome.

I Heard the Owl Call My Name Multiple Choice Test 1 Page 6

IV. Vocabulary: Multiple choice. Write in the letter of the word that matches the definition.

____ 1. CONSENT
____ 2. DEPRIVATION
____ 3. RESENT
____ 4. TAUNTED
____ 5. POIGNANCY
____ 6. TEEMED
____ 7. ANTHROPOLOGIST
____ 8. ANGUISH
____ 9. CALAMITY
____ 10. VAGUE
____ 11. UNAVOIDABLE
____ 12. AGNOSTIC
____ 13. INTERVENE
____ 14. FUTILITY
____ 15. UTTERLY
____ 16. GARRULOUS
____ 17. EERIE
____ 18. SUSTENANCE
____ 19. APPALLING
____ 20. EXASPERATING

A. One who believes neither the existence or nature of God is known
B. Talking much
C. To come between
D. State of being effective, or emotionally touching
E. To feel or express indignant displeasure
F. Indefinite; confused; hazy
G. Loss; hindering from possessing
H. Distress; extreme pain in body or mind
I. Teased; ridiculed
J. Totally
K. Cause to overcome with fear or horror
L. Weird; uncanny
M. Food; nourishment
N. One who studies the science of man
O. Cannot keep away from
P. Inflaming the anger of
Q. Disaster
R. Uselessness
S. Abounded; crowded
T. To agree or give approval

MULTIPLE CHOICE UNIT TEST #2 - *I Heard the Owl Call My Name*

I. Matching/Identify

___ 1. Calamity Bill   A. Chief

___ 2. Bishop   B. Retired canon; helps Mark get started

___ 3. Caleb   C. Village matriarch

___ 4. Jim   D. Goes with Gordon but returns to Jim

___ 5. T. P.   E. Adopts white man's ways & ambitions

___ 6. Eddy   F. Mark scatters his ashes

___ 7. Mrs. Hudson   G. Vicar

___ 8. Keetah   H. Village

___ 9. Peter   I. Takes Mark to Kingcome & becomes his friend

___ 10. Gordon   J. The carver

___ 11. Kingcome   K. Sends Mark to Kingcome

___ 12. Mark   L. Elder of the tribe

II. Multiple Choice

1. What information does the preface reveal?
    a. It tells about the priest's life before he came to the village.
    b. It tells about the young vicar's illness.
    c. It explains the Indian culture.
    d. It tells why the author wrote the book.

2. Before Mark meets the Indians, how does he think they will respond to him?
    a. He thinks they will be cautious but congenial.
    b. He thinks they will be arrogant.
    c. He thinks they will be very friendly.
    d. He thinks they will be wary and unfriendly.

I Heard the Owl Call My Name Multiple Choice Unit Test 2 Page 2

3. Identify the speaker: "If man were to vanish from this planet tomorrow, here he would leave no trace that he ever was."
    a. It was Mark.
    b. It was Jim.
    c. It was Caleb.
    d. It was the bishop.

4. What does it tell us about Mark that he "sensed there was something yet unfinished of which he had no part?"
    a. It shows that he is a procrastinator; he has trouble completing a task.
    b. It shows that he does not make friends easily.
    c. It shows that he is a very fearful, almost paranoid, person.
    d. It illustrates his respect and consideration for the traditions and values of the Indians.

5. What advice does the Bishop write to Mark?
    a. He suggests that Mark leave everything the way it is for at least six months, until the Indians are used to him.
    b. The bishop suggests Mark must work with his hands to gain the respect of the Indians.
    c. He tells Mark to let the Indians do all of the work.
    d. He tells Mark to hire some white men to help with the project.

6. What word is missing in this statement of Mark's? "One kind of _____ is not even being aware that a problem exists. The other kind is the _____ of a man who has searched for answers and discovered that man knows little, yet he retains his convictions and beliefs."
    a. Question
    b. Selfishness
    c. Sin
    d. Naivete

7. What happened when Mark quoted an old Indian prayer that Jim had forgotten?
    a. Jim accepted him as a potential friend because of Mark's interest in the people.
    b. Jim got upset and told Mark never to speak the holy words of the Indians.
    c. Jim was insulted and embarrassed.
    d. Jim got a frightened look on his face and ran away.

8. What does Jim mean when he calls Gordon "fast moving water" and Keetah "the pool?"
    a. These are Gordon and Keetah's other Indian names.
    b. He thinks they will be a good match for each other.
    c. These are the roles Gordon and Keetah have in a tribal ritual.
    d. He thinks they are not well suited for each other.

I Heard the Owl Call My Name Multiple Choice Unit Test 2 Page 3

9. What is the "strange little wind of dissent" that Mark feels?
    a. He had a disagreement with Jim and is worried that their friendship is in jeopardy.
    b. A winter blizzard is approaching.
    c. He thinks the Bishop is displeased with his work.
    d. It is the tension between the old ways and the new.

10. Why is Mrs. Hudson's family leaving the village in shame?
    a. The white man has ridiculed the Indians' customs and refused to have any of them at his wedding.
    b. Her granddaughter and the white man are living together before they are married, and this is not permitted.
    c. Her granddaughter and the white man have bought the valuable mask from Gordon's uncle after getting him drunk.
    d. The white man is a gambler and the Indians do not play cards. They think it is evil.

11. True or False: When Mrs. Hudson talks to Mark and says "What have you done to us?" she is blaming him for her misfortune.
    a. True
    b. False

12. Which statement describes the visitors who come to the village?
    a. They were interested in the Indians as objects of study and amusement, not as people.
    b. They were desperate for food and shelter.
    c. They were tourists just interested in finding a good fishing spot.
    d. They were interested primarily in the Indians as human beings.

13. How do the old people of the village feel about Gordon?
    a. They are jealous of him.
    b. They fear him and his ideas.
    c. They are not particularly concerned. They think he is a foolish young man who will come to his senses.
    d. They accept him for who he is.

14. Marta writes to the Bishop and tells him she is "keeping her promise now." What is her promise?
    a. She has agreed to stay at the vicarage until she retires.
    b. She has trained the young village girls to be good housewives.
    c. She has converted to Christianity.
    d. She has notified the Bishop that Mark's health is failing.

I Heard the Owl Call My Name Multiple Choice Unit Test 2 Page 4

15. What does the Bishop think about life in the villages?
    a. He wonders if anyone there will ever be converted to Christianity.
    b. He dismisses it without much thought.
    c. He thinks the struggles and achievements of life are clearer in the village.
    d. He thinks village life is much more difficult than life elsewhere because of the lack of conveniences.

16. Why did Mark say to Marta, "On the bank of the river I heard the owl call my name?"
    a. He was explaining that he finally felt accepted into the village.
    b. He sensed that he was dying and wanted to know if it were true.
    c. He was delirious with a fever and didn't know what he was talking about.
    d. He was talking symbolically about the blending of the old customs and the modern way of life. He felt like he was the bridge between the two.

17. Which of the following statements describes Mark's life/death?
    a. His death was sudden, like a flame being extinguished.
    b. He lived only through others, like the reflection on the water.
    c. He lived a short yet full, rich life. He died in a triumph of achievement like the swimmer.
    d. His life was hollow, like the wind.

I Heard the Owl Call My Name Multiple Choice Test 2 Page 5

III. Composition
    What is one main idea, one theme from *I Heard the Owl Call My Name*? Explain how that idea is shown in the book.

I Heard the Owl Call My Name Multiple Choice Test 2 Page 6

IV. Vocabulary: Multiple choice. Write in the letter of the word that matches the definition.

____ 1. PIOUS		A. Loss; hindering from possessing
____ 2. TEEMED		B. Distress; extreme pain in body or mind
____ 3. BECKONED		C. Talking much
____ 4. GARRULOUS		D. People banished from their own country
____ 5. CONSENT		E. Embarrassed
____ 6. VICAR		F. To agree or give approval
____ 7. ABASHED		G. Summoned by a gesture
____ 8. TREK		H. Abounded; crowded
____ 9. ANGUISH		I. Disaster
____ 10. UTTERLY		J. Formal installation into office
____ 11. TAUNTED		K. Totally
____ 12. CONFABULATION		L. Clergyman; priest
____ 13. PRECIOUS		M. Of great value
____ 14. INAUGURATION		N. Crucial; sharp; necessary
____ 15. CALAMITY		O. Familiar conversation; chat
____ 16. EXODUS		P. Teased; ridiculed
____ 17. ACUTE		Q. A going out
____ 18. DISSENT		R. To differ in opinion
____ 19. EXILES		S. A journey
____ 20. DEPRIVATION		T. Devout; religious

MULTIPLE CHOICE UNIT TESTS ANSWER SHEET - *I Heard the Owl Call My Name*

I. Matching
1. ___
2. ___
3. ___
4. ___
5. ___
6. ___
7. ___
8. ___
9. ___
10. ___
11. ___
12. ___

II. Multiple Choice

1. (A) (B) (C) (D)
2. (A) (B) (C) (D)
3. (A) (B) (C) (D)
4. (A) (B) (C) (D)
5. (A) (B) (C) (D)
6. (A) (B) (C) (D)
7. (A) (B) (C) (D)
8. (A) (B) (C) (D)
9. (A) (B) (C) (D)
10. (A) (B) (C) (D)
11. (A) (B) (C) (D)
12. (A) (B) (C) (D)
13. (A) (B) (C) (D)
14. (A) (B) (C) (D)
15. (A) (B) (C) (D)
16. (A) (B) (C) (D)
17. (A) (B) (C) (D)

IV. Vocabulary
1. ___
2. ___
3. ___
4. ___
5. ___
6. ___
7. ___
8. ___
9. ___
10. ___
11. ___
12. ___
13. ___
14. ___
15. ___
16. ___
17. ___
18. ___
19. ___
20. ___

ANSWER KEY - *I Heard the Owl Call My Name*
Multiple Choice Unit Test 1

I. Matching
1. F
2. K
3. B
4. I
5. L
6. A
7. C
8. D
9. J
10. E
11. H
12. G

II. Multiple Choice

1. (A) (B) ( ) (D)
2. ( ) (B) (C) (D)
3. (A) (B) (C) ( )
4. ( ) (B) (C) (D)
5. ( ) (B) (C) (D)
6. (A) (B) ( ) (D)
7. (A) ( ) (C) (D)
8. (A) (B) (C) ( )
9. (A) ( ) (C) (D)
10. (A) ( ) (C) (D)
11. (A) ( ) (C) (D)
12. (A) ( ) (C) (D)
13. (A) (B) ( ) (D)
14. (A) (B) ( ) (D)
15. (A) ( ) (C) (D)
16. (A) (B) ( ) (D)
17. ( ) (B) (C) (D)

IV. Vocabulary
1. T
2. G
3. E
4. I
5. D
6. S
7. N
8. H
9. Q
10. F
11. O
12. A
13. C
14. R
15. J
16. B
17. L
18. M
19. K
20. P

ANSWER KEY - *I Heard the Owl Call My Name*
Multiple Choice Unit Test 2

I. Matching
1. D
2. E
3. L
4. I
5. B
6. G
7. J
8. F
9. C
10. K
11. H
12. A

II. Multiple Choice

1. (A) ( ) (C) (D)
2. (A) ( ) (C) (D)
3. ( ) (B) (C) (D)
4. (A) (B) (C) ( )
5. (A) ( ) (C) (D)
6. (A) (B) (C) ( )
7. ( ) (B) (C) (D)
8. (A) (B) (C) ( )
9. (A) (B) (C) ( )
10. (A) (B) ( ) (D)
11. (A) ( ) (C) (D)
12. ( ) (B) (C) (D)
13. (A) ( ) (C) (D)
14. (A) (B) (C) ( )
15. (A) (B) ( ) (D)
16. (A) ( ) (C) (D)
17. (A) (B) ( ) (D)

IV. Vocabulary
1. T
2. H
3. G
4. C
5. F
6. L
7. E
8. S
9. B
10. K
11. P
12. O
13. M
14. J
15. I
16. Q
17. N
18. R
19. D
20. A

UNIT RESOURCE MATERIALS

BULLETIN BOARD IDEAS - *I Heard the Owl Call My Name*

1. Save one corner of the board for the best of students' *I Heard the Owl Call My Name* writing assignments.

2. Take one of the word search puzzles from the extra activities packet and with a marker copy it over in a large size on the bulletin board. Write the clue words to find to one side. Invite students prior to and after class to find the words and circle them on the bulletin board.

3. Display maps and pictures of the British Columbia.

4. Make a bulletin board about missionaries and the places they work.

5. Display articles and pictures about the various Indian tribes of the Northwest. Perhaps you could incorporate students' writing assignments.

6. Place a map of North America on the bulletin board. Place a cut-out owl over the area where the story takes place.

7. Use a story line to show Mark's assimilation into the Indian culture.

8. Put up pictures of things from the story: an owl, a salmon run, a mask, a vicarage in the woods, etc. Title the board I HEARD THE OWL CALL MY NAME.

9. Post recent articles about minority cultures in this country showing current issues relating to minorities.

10. Do a bulletin board about careers students could have relating to the story: missionary, someone who works in Indian relations, teacher, woodworker, etc.

EXTRA ACTIVITIES - *I Heard The Owl Call My Name*

One of the difficulties in teaching a novel is that all students don't read at the same speed. One student who likes to read may take the book home and finish it in a day or two. Sometimes a few students finish the in-class assignments early. The problem, then, is finding suitable extra activities for students.

One thing that helps is to keep a little library in the classroom. For this unit on *I Heard the Owl Call My Name*, you might check out from the school library other related books and articles about North American Indians, the Northwestern wilderness areas, mission work, minority rights and responsibilities, current issues regarding North American Indians and other minority cultures, or articles of criticism about Margaret Craven's work.

Other things you may keep on hand are puzzles. We have made some relating directly to *I Heard the Owl Call My Name* for you. Feel free to duplicate them.

Some students may like to draw. You might devise a contest or allow some extra-credit grade for students who draw characters or scenes from *I Heard the Owl Call My Name*. Note, too, that if the students do not want to keep their drawings you may pick up some extra bulletin board materials this way. If you have a contest and you supply the prize (a CD or something like that perhaps), you could, possibly, make the drawing itself a non-returnable entry fee.

The pages which follow contain games, puzzles and worksheets. The keys, when appropriate, immediately follow the puzzle or worksheet. There are two main groups of activities: one group for the unit; that is, generally relating to *I Heard the Owl Call My Name* text, and another group of activities related strictly to *I Heard the Owl Call My Name* vocabulary.

Directions for these games, puzzles and worksheets are self-explanatory. The object here is to provide you with extra materials you may use in any way you choose.

MORE ACTIVITIES - *I Heard the Owl Call My Name*

1. Have students design a book cover for *I Heard the Owl Call My Name* (front and back and inside flaps).

2. Have students design a bulletin board (ready to be put up; not just sketched) for *I Heard the Owl Call My Name.*

3. Use some of the related topics (noted earlier for an in-class library) as topics for research, reports or written papers, or as topics for guest speakers.

4. As an alternate introductory activity, prepare a bulletin board titled "Tips for Making a Successful Life." During the introductory lesson, have students brainstorm what it means to have a successful life, and things they can do to help make their own lives successful. Write their suggestions on the bulletin board.

5. Have students research cultures within cultures. Each student should pick one culture within a culture and research its heritage, problems, and successes.

6. Have students construct a map of the way they think Kingcome Village looked.

7. Discuss family traditions -- things your students' families do for holidays, birthdays, vacations, or any time they do something special that is a tradition. Also include a discussion of traditions that have gone by the wayside through the years.

8. In the book, it says Mark learned how to live and how to die. Ask students what that means, and exactly what Mark learned. What does it mean to live, and what does it mean to die?

WORD SEARCH - *I Heard the Owl Call My Name*

All words in this list are associated with *I Heard the Owl Call My Name*. The words are placed backwards, forward, diagonally, up and down. The included words are listed below the word search.

```
M N H E Y N D B A H G T W Z M D X C L L J C D W
J P R E Y K O E J P U R C K H A I M Z Z H P B Q
G X Q A L E L T I J E D A S W T R G F E V A Q F
T U R N I P S M S R O T S E C N A K N I G H T S
X P T J K N I N H A R M E O B A W O C I T X S C
W P E T J J A R F E K A H R N A L A G A T L B C
L F M D E I Z X E V W C M B K A R E E O T Y L Q
B O A T D R E N D X L Z U W M A N D B W R N J M
H R Z N B Y C L K X B R A L G S E I D E E D B R
V C I E K V Z D R S I L L E G Y S G V V Y G O J
C D H A T E E K T A A S Y W D H Y U A J S A M N
F A S Z N H I N L V C M C C O L O R F R F Z Q K
K S L S N N E C J K B Y C P L C C W E M U N D H
M J Q A G S A L M O N T P U N T D D V C O O C Z
H D V C M Q S T K J H R G A N R L J V X S T C Z
T V O K T I F K L J V L V E X E Q M K W A B O S
F M Z M K Z T X R M B P S C P B J D G L K F M R
E S Y T C Q X Y D V R S M V R S V P T S Y B L C
W Q M C W T Q T V B I F Z F T W S O R C W G S L
Y T C T V R R S B D F T J N D T P H K N Y W L G
```

ALONE	DISSENT	INDIANS	PLEA
ANCESTORS	EDDY	JIM	POTLATCH
BEAR	ELDERS	KEETAH	RAIN
BISHOP	END	KINGCOME	SALMON
BOAT	ETHEL	KNIGHTS	SAM
BRIAN	EYES	KWAKWALA	TP
BURIAL	GLUCKASTON	MAN	TREE
CALAMITY	GORDON	MARK	TURNIPS
CALEB	GULLY	MARRIED	VANCOUVER
COURAGE	GUTTER	MASK	VICARAGE
CRAVEN	HAT	MOTOR	WE
DEATH	HELP	OWL	
DIGNITY	HUDSON	PETER	

KEY: WORD SEARCH - *I Heard the Owl Call My Name*

All words in this list are associated with *I Heard the Owl Call My Name*. The words are placed backwards, forward, diagonally, up and down. The included words are listed below the word searches.

```
            H E   N D   A H         M D
            R E Y   O E   P U R     A I         H
    G       A L E L T I   E D A   W   R G   E V A
    T U R N I P S M S R O T S E C N A K N I G H T S
        T     N I N   A R   E O B A W O C   I T
        E T     J A     E K A   R N A L A G A T
          D E I       E       C M B K A R E E O     Y
    B O A T D R E N D         U W M A N D B   R N
        R   N   Y     K   R A L G   E I   E E D
          I E         S I L L E G   S G V V           O
    C   H A T E E K   A A       W   H Y U A   S A M N
      A     N H I     L     M       O L O R
        L     N E               P L C C   E M U         H
              A G S A L M O N T P U N T   D       O O C
              C M                 G A N   L           T C
          O     I                 V E   E           A   O
        M       T                 S                 L   R
      E           Y         S               T
                          I                     O
                        D                     P
```

ALONE
ANCESTORS
BEAR
BISHOP
BOAT
BRIAN
BURIAL
CALAMITY
CALEB
COURAGE
CRAVEN
DEATH
DIGNITY

DISSENT
EDDY
ELDERS
END
ETHEL
EYES
GLUCKASTON
GORDON
GULLY
GUTTER
HAT
HELP
HUDSON

INDIANS
JIM
KEETAH
KINGCOME
KNIGHTS
KWAKWALA
MAN
MARK
MARRIED
MASK
MOTOR
OWL
PETER

PLEA
POTLATCH
RAIN
SALMON
SAM
TP
TREE
TURNIPS
VANCOUVER
VICARAGE
WE

CROSSWORD - *I Heard the Owl Call My Name*

CROSSWORD CLUES - *I Heard The Owl Call My Name*

ACROSS
1. Village
4. Sent Mark to Kingcome
8. There is a ---- loose in the church
9. Stop; terminate
12. False god
14. Old villagers who decide things
15. Goals; aspirations
17. Village drunk and wife beater
18. Marta made one for Mark
20. Natives
22. Aid
25. By yourself
26. Ingest food
28. If ___ were to vanish from this planet tomorrow, here he would leave no trace
29. Elder of the tribe
31. Traditional burial place
32. The watchful waiting left the Indian's ___
33. Decays
35. Belonging to it
36. Priest; clergyman
37. Author
39. Adopted white man's ways & ambitions
40. Feast with gifts
44. English phrase 'Thank you' doesn't exist in this language
46. Bravery
47. Coordinating conjunction
48. Thin
49. City where Keetah's sister died

DOWN
1. Went with Gordon but returned to Jim
2. Retired Canon; helped Mark get started
3. Victorian expression meaning 'you'
4. Mark's last name
5. The swimmer
6. I Heard the ___ Call My Name
7. Bill; Mark scatters his ashes
8. The RCMP officer issues ___ permits
10. Opposite of life
11. Chief
13. Mark felt a 'strange little wind of ___'
16. River transportation
19. ___ Inlet; where Mark promised to spread ashes
21. Self-respect
23. Mark pulled her tooth
24. The carver
25. One's past relatives
27. Where the church does its best work
28. Vicar
30. Ask in earnest
34. Mark's house
38. Boat engine
39. Ditch made by heavy rains
41. A single
42. Heirloom sold too cheaply
43. Water from the sky
45. Opposite of lose

CROSSWORD - *I Heard the Owl Call My Name*

MATCHING QUIZ/WORKSHEET 1 - *I Heard the Owl Call My Name*

____ 1. JIM   A. Village drunk and wife beater

____ 2. MARRIED   B. Mark's house

____ 3. SAM   C. English phrase 'Thank you' doesn't exist in this language

____ 4. TREE   D. Jim and Keetah get ____

____ 5. POTLATCH   E. One's past relatives

____ 6. VANCOUVER   F. Feast with gifts

____ 7. CALEB   G. Retired Canon; helped Mark get started

____ 8. VICARAGE   H. Opposite of life

____ 9. PETER   I. Village

____ 10. MOTOR   J. By yourself

____ 11. ANCESTORS   K. Traditional burial place

____ 12. BRIAN   L. Boat engine

____ 13. KEETAH   M. Victorian expression meaning 'you'

____ 14. WE   N. City where Keetah's sister died

____ 15. KINGCOME   O. The carver

____ 16. ALONE   P. Chief

____ 17. HUDSON   Q. Took Mark to Kingcome & became his friend

____ 18. KWAKWALA   R. Mark's last name

____ 19. EDDY   S. Went with Gordon but returned to Jim

____ 20. DEATH   T. Village matriarch

KEY: MATCHING QUIZ/WORKSHEET 1 - *I Heard the Owl Call My Name*

_Q_	1. JIM	A. Village drunk and wife beater
_D_	2. MARRIED	B. Mark's house
_A_	3. SAM	C. English phrase 'Thank you' doesn't exist in this language
_K_	4. TREE	D. Jim and Keetah get ____
_F_	5. POTLATCH	E. One's past relatives
_N_	6. VANCOUVER	F. Feast with gifts
_G_	7. CALEB	G. Retired Canon; helped Mark get started
_B_	8. VICARAGE	H. Opposite of life
_O_	9. PETER	I. Village
_L_	10. MOTOR	J. By yourself
_E_	11. ANCESTORS	K. Traditional burial place
_R_	12. BRIAN	L. Boat engine
_S_	13. KEETAH	M. Victorian expression meaning 'you'
_M_	14. WE	N. City where Keetah's sister died
_I_	15. KINGCOME	O. The carver
_J_	16. ALONE	P. Chief
_T_	17. HUDSON	Q. Took Mark to Kingcome & became his friend
_C_	18. KWAKWALA	R. Mark's last name
_P_	19. EDDY	S. Went with Gordon but returned to Jim
_H_	20. DEATH	T. Village matriarch

MATCHING QUIZ/WORKSHEET 2 - *I Heard the Owl Call My Name*

____ 1. MASK   A. Marta made one for Mark

____ 2. OWL   B. The RCMP officer issues ___ permits

____ 3. ETHEL   C. Mark's house

____ 4. KINGCOME   D. Village

____ 5. CALEB   E. If ___ were to vanish from this planet tomorrow, here he would leave no trace

____ 6. DIGNITY   F. Heirloom sold too cheaply

____ 7. HELP   G. The watchful waiting left the Indian's ___

____ 8. GULLY   H. Jim and Keetah get ____

____ 9. BEAR   I. Mrs. Hudson's small revenge

____ 10. HUDSON   J. Aid

____ 11. BURIAL   K. Natives

____ 12. INDIANS   L. Village matriarch

____ 13. VICARAGE   M. Mark pulled her tooth

____ 14. EYES   N. There is a ---- loose in the church

____ 15. ANCESTORS   O. Self-respect

____ 16. MAN   P. Village drunk and wife beater

____ 17. HAT   Q. Ditch made by heavy rains

____ 18. MARRIED   R. I Heard the ___ Call My Name

____ 19. TURNIPS   S. One's past relatives

____ 20. SAM   T. Retired Canon; helped Mark get started

KEY: MATCHING QUIZ/WORKSHEET 2 - *I Heard the Owl Call My Name*

_F_	1. MASK	A. Marta made one for Mark
_R_	2. OWL	B. The RCMP officer issues ___ permits
_M_	3. ETHEL	C. Mark's house
_D_	4. KINGCOME	D. Village
_T_	5. CALEB	E. If ___ were to vanish from this planet tomorrow, here he would leave no trace
_O_	6. DIGNITY	F. Heirloom sold too cheaply
_J_	7. HELP	G. The watchful waiting left the Indian's ___
_Q_	8. GULLY	H. Jim and Keetah get ___
_N_	9. BEAR	I. Mrs. Hudson's small revenge
_L_	10. HUDSON	J. Aid
_B_	11. BURIAL	K. Natives
_K_	12. INDIANS	L. Village matriarch
_C_	13. VICARAGE	M. Mark pulled her tooth
_G_	14. EYES	N. There is a ---- loose in the church
_S_	15. ANCESTORS	O. Self-respect
_E_	16. MAN	P. Village drunk and wife beater
_A_	17. HAT	Q. Ditch made by heavy rains
_H_	18. MARRIED	R. I Heard the ___ Call My Name
_I_	19. TURNIPS	S. One's past relatives
_P_	20. SAM	T. Retired Canon; helped Mark get started

JUGGLE LETTER REVIEW GAME CLUE SHEET - *I Heard the Owl Call My Name*

SCRAMBLED	WORD	CLUE
NOELA	ALONE	By yourself
STANROSCE	ANCESTORS	One's past relatives
RABE	BEAR	There is a ---- loose in the church
BOSPHI	BISHOP	Sent Mark to Kingcome
ATBO	BOAT	River transportation
INRAB	BRIAN	Mark's last name
LABURI	BURIAL	The RCMP officer issues ___ permits
MATALYIC	CALAMITY	Bill; Mark scatters his ashes
CLABE	CALEB	Retired Canon; helped Mark get started
GOCAREU	COURAGE	Bravery
VANCER	CRAVEN	Author
TADEH	DEATH	Opposite of life
GITINYD	DIGNITY	Self-respect
SIDENST	DISSENT	Mark felt a 'strange little wind of ___'
YEDD	EDDY	Chief
SLEEDR	ELDERS	Old villagers who decide things
NED	END	Stop; terminate
TEELH	ETHEL	Mark pulled her tooth
SEEY	EYES	The watchful waiting left the Indian's ___
KUSANTLOCG	GLUCKASTON	Seaweed and corn dinner
DOONRG	GORDON	Adopted white man's ways & ambitions
YULLG	GULLY	Ditch made by heavy rains
TURGET	GUTTER	Where the church does its best work
THA	HAT	Marta made one for Mark
PHEL	HELP	Aid
NUSHOD	HUDSON	Village matriarch
SADININ	INDIANS	Natives
MIJ	JIM	Took Mark to Kingcome & became his friend
HATKEE	KEETAH	Went with Gordon but returned to Jim
MIGCENOK	KINGCOME	Village
NGTSKIH	KNIGHTS	____ Inlet; where Mark promised to spread ashes
WWKKLAAA	KWAKWALA	English phrase 'Thank you' doesn't exist in this language
NAM	MAN	If ___ were to vanish from this planet tomorrow, here he would leave no trace
KMAR	MARK	Vicar
RIDERAM	MARRIED	Jim and Keetah get ____
SKAM	MASK	Heirloom sold too cheaply
ROOMT	MOTOR	Boat engine
WOL	OWL	I Heard the ___ Call My Name
PREET	PETER	The carver
LEAP	PLEA	Ask in earnest
LOCHTAPT	POTLATCH	Feast with gifts

Vocabulary Juggle Letter Review Game Clues Continued

NAIR	RAIN	Water from the sky
LANOMS	SALMON	The swimmer
MAS	SAM	Village drunk and wife beater
PT	TP	Elder of the tribe
RETE	TREE	Traditional burial place
NUSTPIR	TURNIPS	Mrs. Hudson's small revenge
CROVNAVU	VANCOUVER	City where Keetah's sister died
RIVECAGA	VICARAGE	Mark's house
EW	WE	Victorian expression meaning 'you'

VOCABULARY RESOURCE MATERIALS

VOCABULARY WORD SEARCH - *I Heard the Owl Call My Name*

All words in this list are associated with *I Heard the Owl Call My Name*. The words are placed backwards, forward, diagonally, up and down. The included words are listed below the word searches.

```
A N G U I S H P A F R T B R H B D S M K L W Y L
S D J L S F Y P K Q S Z X G E S X E W K N S J T
M U D U B Y P M T M W U K K W A P B N W P T R L
S U O I C A C I F F E U S R U P S U D O X E V V
E I S U L H G E R U A W D T P A T S T Y K J D B
P X Q L T V W N X E T N D E E L P U E E J C J C
C G I V I C A R O A S I T I M N A P X R E Y E X
D N X L K C N G C S S E L H N E A T A V T R M B
G E P K E H O U U S T P N I R A E N I L L I I J
I A P O D S T N E E G I E T T O N T C T L S N E
X N N R I E L N S C N E C R K Y P I H E U E N G
M V T A I G T V E E A G N C A E A O M O Q D D C
P X M E C V N N Q N N L Q T C T F B L A C J E K
X R Z Q R H A A U S M T A R I J I U A O T F Z S
N T E Y G V R T N A Q I E M V L R N Z S G E Y G
V V F C M L E O I C T P T W I R I G G H H I K W
T G Z T I M F N N O Y P V Y A T K T X C N E S V
M R Q V S O D D E I N P B G G W Y T Y W N S D T
V T C D D G U J F X S H H V G V L F B V T X T R
U T T E R L Y S Z K B M U N A V O I D A B L E H
```

ABASHED	CONSENT	GENTILITY	SUSTENANCE
ACUTE	DEPRIVATION	INANIMATE	TAUNTED
AGNOSTIC	DISSENT	INTERVENE	TEEMED
ANACHRONISM	EERIE	PERCEPTIVE	TREK
ANGUISH	EFFICACIOUS	PIOUS	UNAVOIDABLE
ANTHROPOLOGIST	ENMITY	PLATITUDES	UNCTUOUS
APPALLED	EXASPERATING	POIGNANCY	UTTERLY
APPALLING	EXILES	PRECIOUS	VAGUE
AUTOPSY	EXODUS	PURSUE	VICAR
BECKONED	FUTILITY	REASSERTING	
CALAMITY	GARRULOUS	RESENT	

KEY: VOCABULARY WORD SEARCH - *I Heard the Owl Call My Name*

All words in this list are associated with *I Heard the Owl Call My Name*. The words are placed backwards, forward, diagonally, up and down. The included words are listed below the word searches.

```
        A N G U I S H   A               R       D                   Y
      S         S     P       S           E       E             S T
          U   U     P           U           A       N     P       R
      S U O I C A C I F F E U S R U P S U D O X E
      E I     U L   G E R U A   D T P A     S T     K
      P X     L T V   N X E T N D E E L P U E E     C
              I V I C A R O A S I T I M N A P   R E     E
      D N     L   C N G C S S E L H N E A T A V T R     B
      G E P     E   O U U S T P N I R A E N I L     I I
      I A P O D S T N E E G I E T T O N T C T L S N E
        N N R I E   N S C     E C R   Y P I     E U E     G
          T A I G T     E E A   N   A E A O M     D D
      P       E C V N N     N N L   T C T     B L A         E
        R       R H A A U     M T A R I     I U A O T         S
            E       V R T N A     I E M     L R N   S G E
                C     E O I C T P T     I R I     G   H I
                    I       N N O Y       Y A T     T         E S
                          O     E I N       G     Y   Y         D T
                                U           S
      U T T E R L Y S         M U N A V O I D A B L E
```

ABASHED	CONSENT	GENTILITY	SUSTENANCE
ACUTE	DEPRIVATION	INANIMATE	TAUNTED
AGNOSTIC	DISSENT	INTERVENE	TEEMED
ANACHRONISM	EERIE	PERCEPTIVE	TREK
ANGUISH	EFFICACIOUS	PIOUS	UNAVOIDABLE
ANTHROPOLOGIST	ENMITY	PLATITUDES	UNCTUOUS
APPALLED	EXASPERATING	POIGNANCY	UTTERLY
APPALLING	EXILES	PRECIOUS	VAGUE
AUTOPSY	EXODUS	PURSUE	VICAR
BECKONED	FUTILITY	REASSERTING	
CALAMITY	GARRULOUS	RESENT	

VOCABULARY CROSSWORD - *I Heard the Owl Call My Name*

VOCABULARY CROSSWORD - *I Heard the Owl Call My Name*

ACROSS

3. Summoned by a gesture
6. Something out of place in point of time
11. If ___ were to vanish from this planet tomorrow, here he would leave no trace
12. To follow or chase
14. There is a ---- loose in the church
15. Teased; ridiculed
17. Victorian expression meaning 'you'
18. Every one
20. Elder of the tribe
21. Opposite of bottom
22. Village drunk and wife beater
23. Devout; religious
24. Marta made one for Mark
25. Crucial; sharp; necessary
27. Fishing strings
28. Aid
29. To agree or give approval
33. The carver
34. Ask in earnest
35. Ditch made by heavy rains
36. Stop; terminate
37. The watchful waiting left the Indian's ___
38. I Heard the ___ Call My Name
39. Hopes; aspirations
40. Indefinite; confused; hazy
43. Loss; hindering from possessing
49. Opposite of life
51. Boat engine
52. Embarrassed
53. Opposite of young
54. Things we learn or are taught

DOWN

1. Took Mark to Kingcome & became his friend
2. One who studies the science of man
4. Hatred; hostility
5. Weird; uncanny
6. Distress; extreme pain in body or mind
7. One who believes neither the existence or nature of God is known
8. To feel or express indignant displeasure
9. Food; nourishment
10. Uselessness
13. Dissection of a dead body to learn the cause of death
16. To differ in opinion
19. Sent Mark to Kingcome
25. Overcome with fear or horror
26. Abounded; crowded
29. Disaster
30. Effective
31. A journey
32. Chief
35. Adopted white man's ways & ambitions
41. People banished from their own country
42. Traditional burial place
44. Mark pulled her tooth
45. Water from the sky
46. Clergyman; priest
47. This day
48. By yourself
50. Unusual

VOCABULARY CROSSWORD - *I Heard the Owl Call My Name*

VOCABULARY WORKSHEET 1 - *I Heard the Owl Call My Name*

____ 1. Formal installation into office
    A. Futility   B. Anachronism   C. Inauguration   D. Unctuous

____ 2. Sentimental pretense of spirituality in speech or attitude
    A. Unctuous   B. Pious   C. Platitudes   D. Acute

____ 3. One who believes neither the existence or nature of God is known
    A. Agnostic   B. Gentility   C. Intervene   D. Acute

____ 4. Discerning; having intuitive judgment
    A. Anachronism   B. Garrulous   C. Vicar   D. Perceptive

____ 5. Of great value
    A. Eerie   B. Resent   C. Precious   D. Unctuous

____ 6. Crucial; sharp; necessary
    A. Dissent   B. Acute   C. Efficacious   D. Taunted

____ 7. People banished from their own country
    A. Futility   B. Anachronism   C. Exiles   D. Consent

____ 8. Reclaiming one's rights or position
    A. Taunted   B. Reasserting   C. Vague   D. Exodus

____ 9. Familiar conversation; chat
    A. Confabulation   B. Pious   C. Agnostic   D. Taunted

____ 10. Teased; ridiculed
    A. Consent   B. Taunted   C. Unctuous   D. Trek

____ 11. A going out
    A. Deprivation   B. Inanimate   C. Exodus   D. Pursue

____ 12. Effective
    A. Efficacious   B. Teemed   C. Confabulation   D. Exodus

____ 13. Trite, commonplace speech; dull or stale truisms
    A. Gentility   B. Platitudes   C. Pious   D. Beckoned

____ 14. Talking much
    A. Appalled   B. Eerie   C. Beckoned   D. Garrulous

____ 15. Indefinite; confused; hazy
    A. Pursue   B. Poignancy   C. Anthropologist   D. Vague

____ 16. Something out of place in point of time
    A. Pursue   B. Anachronism   C. Abashed   D. Autopsy

____ 17. Distress; extreme pain in body or mind
    A. Anguish   B. Dissent   C. Anachronism   D. Reasserting

____ 18. To differ in opinion
    A. Enmity   B. Abashed   C. Dissent   D. Appalling

____ 19. State of being effective, or emotionally touching
    A. Exodus   B. Exiles   C. Poignancy   D. Perceptive

____ 20. To come between
    A. Deprivation   B. Platitudes   C. Acute   D. Intervene

KEY: VOCABULARY WORKSHEET 1 - *I Heard the Owl Call My Name*

__C__ 1. Formal installation into office
    A. Futility   B. Anachronism   C. Inauguration   D. Unctuous

__C__ 2. Sentimental pretense of spirituality in speech or attitude
    A. Unctuous   B. Pious   C. Platitudes   D. Acute

__A__ 3. One who believes neither the existence or nature of God is known
    A. Agnostic   B. Gentility   C. Intervene   D. Acute

__D__ 4. Discerning; having intuitive judgment
    A. Anachronism   B. Garrulous   C. Vicar   D. Perceptive

__C__ 5. Of great value
    A. Eerie   B. Resent   C. Precious   D. Unctuous

__B__ 6. Crucial; sharp; necessary
    A. Dissent   B. Acute   C. Efficacious   D. Taunted

__C__ 7. People banished from their own country
    A. Futility   B. Anachronism   C. Exiles   D. Consent

__B__ 8. Reclaiming one's rights or position
    A. Taunted   B. Reasserting   C. Vague   D. Exodus

__A__ 9. Familiar conversation; chat
    A. Confabulation   B. Pious   C. Agnostic   D. Taunted

__B__ 10. Teased; ridiculed
    A. Consent   B. Taunted   C. Unctuous   D. Trek

__C__ 11. A going out
    A. Deprivation   B. Inanimate   C. Exodus   D. Pursue

__A__ 12. Effective
    A. Efficacious   B. Teemed   C. Confabulation   D. Exodus

__B__ 13. Trite, commonplace speech; dull or stale truisms
    A. Gentility   B. Platitudes   C. Pious   D. Beckoned

__D__ 14. Talking much
    A. Appalled   B. Eerie   C. Beckoned   D. Garrulous

__D__ 15. Indefinite; confused; hazy
    A. Pursue   B. Poignancy   C. Anthropologist   D. Vague

__B__ 16. Something out of place in point of time
    A. Pursue   B. Anachronism   C. Abashed   D. Autopsy

__A__ 17. Distress; extreme pain in body or mind
    A. Anguish   B. Dissent   C. Anachronism   D. Reasserting

__C__ 18. To differ in opinion
    A. Enmity   B. Abashed   C. Dissent   D. Appalling

__C__ 19. State of being effective, or emotionally touching
    A. Exodus   B. Exiles   C. Poignancy   D. Perceptive

__D__ 20. To come between
    A. Deprivation   B. Platitudes   C. Acute   D. Intervene

VOCABULARY WORKSHEET 2 - *I Heard the Owl Call My Name*

____ 1. FUTILITY   A. Distress; extreme pain in body or mind

____ 2. ANTHROPOLOGIST   B. To agree or give approval

____ 3. APPALLED   C. To feel or express indignant displeasure

____ 4. EXASPERATING   D. Totally

____ 5. ABASHED   E. Qualities appropriate to those well-born

____ 6. PRECIOUS   F. A journey

____ 7. ANGUISH   G. Discerning; having intuitive judgment

____ 8. PERCEPTIVE   H. Formal installation into office

____ 9. EERIE   I. One who studies the science of man

____ 10. UTTERLY   J. Of great value

____ 11. TEEMED   K. Embarrassed

____ 12. APPALLING   L. People banished from their own country

____ 13. GENTILITY   M. Overcome with fear or horror

____ 14. DISSENT   N. Weird; uncanny

____ 15. CONSENT   O. Cause to overcome with fear or horror

____ 16. SUSTENANCE   P. Abounded; crowded

____ 17. INAUGURATION   Q. Inflaming the anger of

____ 18. EXILES   R. Uselessness

____ 19. RESENT   S. Food; nourishment

____ 20. TREK   T. To differ in opinion

- I Heard the Owl Call My Name

__R_	1. FUTILITY	A. Distress; extreme pain in body or mind
__I_	2. ANTHROPOLOGIST	B. To agree or give approval
__M_	3. APPALLED	C. To feel or express indignant displeasure
__Q_	4. EXASPERATING	D. Totally
__K_	5. ABASHED	E. Qualities appropriate to those well-born
__J_	6. PRECIOUS	F. A journey
__A_	7. ANGUISH	G. Discerning; having intuitive judgment
__G_	8. PERCEPTIVE	H. Formal installation into office
__N_	9. EERIE	I. One who studies the science of man
__D_	10. UTTERLY	J. Of great value
__P_	11. TEEMED	K. Embarrassed
__O_	12. APPALLING	L. People banished from their own country
__E_	13. GENTILITY	M. Overcome with fear or horror
__T_	14. DISSENT	N. Weird; uncanny
__B_	15. CONSENT	O. Cause to overcome with fear or horror
__S_	16. SUSTENANCE	P. Abounded; crowded
__H_	17. INAUGURATION	Q. Inflaming the anger of
__L_	18. EXILES	R. Uselessness
__C_	19. RESENT	S. Food; nourishment
__F_	20. TREK	T. To differ in opinion

VOCABULARY JUGGLE LETTER REVIEW GAME CLUES - *I Heard the Owl Call My Name*

SCRAMBLED	WORD	CLUE
SBADAHE	ABASHED	Embarrassed
TUAEC	ACUTE	Crucial; sharp; necessary
SATIGONC	AGNOSTIC	One who believes neither the existence or nature of God is known
HOMACNNRISA	ANACHRONISM	Something out of place in point of time
GHINUSA	ANGUISH	Distress; extreme pain in body or mind
HOGNOTTOLRISA	ANTHROPOLOGIST	One who studies the science of man
LEDPAPLA	APPALLED	Overcome with fear or horror
LIGPLANAP	APPALLING	Cause to overcome with fear or horror
STOPYAU	AUTOPSY	Dissection of a dead body to learn the cause of death
KEBOCDNE	BECKONED	Summoned by a gesture
AYILMACT	CALAMITY	Disaster
TONBALAFCOUN	CONFABULATION	Familiar conversation; chat
TONCNES	CONSENT	To agree or give approval
RAVEDNIPTIO	DEPRIVATION	Loss; hindering from possessing
SIDNETS	DISSENT	To differ in opinion
REEEI	EERIE	Weird; uncanny
FOCCSUFIAIE	EFFICACIOUS	Effective
MYNEIT	ENMITY	Hatred; hostility
INRAXTEPGEAS	EXASPERATING	Inflaming the anger of
ILEEXS	EXILES	People banished from their own country
OXSEDU	EXODUS	A going out
YUFILITT	FUTILITY	Uselessness
GLUSROAUR	GARRULOUS	Talking much
IYGTINLET	GENTILITY	Qualities appropriate to those well-born
MANINAETI	INANIMATE	Lifeless
NUNRUGTOAAII	INAUGURATION	Formal installation into office
VINTNEER	INTERVENE	To come between
VIPPCEETER	PERCEPTIVE	Discerning; having intuitive judgment
SOUPI	PIOUS	Devout; religious
LUSTIDAPTE	PLATITUDES	Trite, commonplace speech; dull or stale truisms
ICOGPANNY	POIGNANCY	State of being effective, or emotionally touching
SRUIEPOC	PRECIOUS	Of great value
ERUPSU	PURSUE	To follow or chase
STEERGRASIN	REASSERTING	Reclaiming one's rights or position
NESTER	RESENT	To feel or express indignant displeasure
USSNNECATE	SUSTENANCE	Food; nourishment
UNDEATT	TAUNTED	Teased; ridiculed
MEETED	TEEMED	Abounded; crowded
RKET	TREK	A journey
INBADEVLOAU	UNAVOIDABLE	Cannot keep away from